What Your Colleagues Are Saying . . .

"Lyle Kirtman not only has deep experience in many facets of education, but he also has a unique ability to think both quantitatively and qualitatively. In *Shaping the Future*, Kirtman provides actionable strategies for creating sustainable student success and empowered educational teams."

Peter DeWitt
Author, Facilitator, Coach, Instructional Leadership Collective
Albany, New York

"*Shaping the Future* is a powerful guide for educators seeking to create a culture of high expectations. By focusing on individual student needs, fostering a supportive environment, and building community partnerships, Kirtman provides a practical and inspiring road map. This book is a must-read for education leaders committed to student success."

Tom Vander Ark
CEO, Getting Smart
Former Executive Director, Bill and Melinda Gates Foundation
Federal Way, Washington

"*Shaping the Future* provides educational leaders with sound and practical advice on how to shift their work so that they can meet the needs of their students and staff and stay relevant. For leaders who seek to lead rather than react to change, this book is essential reading."

Pedro A. Noguera
Dean, Rossier School of Education
Distinguished Professor of Education
Los Angeles, California

"Kirtman makes the thoughtful and crucial case for shifting our thinking and practice for the good of all students. It is not for a lack of trying that American public education has not moved the needle on student success—but we need a new north star and this book is a great beginning."

David P. Driscoll
Former Massachusetts Commissioner of Education
Melrose, Massachusetts

"Kirtman cuts through the noise of the times, providing us with very relevant, practical, researched-based steps to help lead and shape the futures of those we serve. He captures the moment we are in and gives us a roadmap to rediscover our north star, thereby guiding us to lead our schools through these rough seas to safer shores."

Kevin Brown
Executive Director, Texas Association of
School Administrators (TASA)
Austin, Texas

"Kirtman focuses on two things that matter the most to educators, simplifying the work and empowering, collaborative leadership. This book is an excellent resource for school leaders seeking a path to success. By pivoting as he suggests, everyone wins."

Kate Dias
President, Connecticut Education Association
Hartford, Connecticut

"*Shaping the Future* challenges us to rethink what effective leadership looks like and who we trust to lead. By uncovering biases that limit innovation and emphasizing traits like persistence, flexibility, and intrinsic accountability, Kirtman offers a bold framework to align leadership with student success. This book isn't just a guide—it's a wake-up call to build schools where everyone rises."

Sherida Britt
Education Strategist
Upper Marlboro, Maryland

"Kirtman is a genius. He gets inside the weeds of organizational change. Not only does he extricate us from the constraints for change, but he also liberates us from the daily grind. If you want novel, high leverage levers for changing cultures using existing hidden forces this is the book for you."

Michael Fullan
Professor Emeritus
Ontario, Canada

"*Shaping the Future* empowers educational leaders with practical and equity-driven guidance to transform their work in ways that address the diverse needs of students and staff. The insights offered are both compelling and actionable, reflecting Kirtman's deep understanding that effective leadership requires clarity, preparation, and a willingness to rethink traditional approaches."

Sinthia Sone-Moyano
Deputy Commissioner, Educational Supports and Wellness
Connecticut State Department of Education
Hartford, Connecticut

Shaping the Future

Dedication

I am dedicating this book to Dr. Robert S. Peterkin, who recently passed away. Bob was my first real mentor and taught me about leadership at an early part of my career. He showed me that leadership was about commitment, courage, humility, and learning how to navigate politics. He said as a young educational leader, I had talent but did not understand politics. He said lucky for me that he could teach me politics. Those lessons saved my career many times, and I have passed on his coaching to many other young leaders. Thank you, Bob, for launching my career along with so many others.

Shaping the Future

Four Leadership Pivots for Lasting Educational Impact

Lyle Kirtman

CORWIN

CORWIN

FOR INFORMATION:

Corwin
A SAGE Company
2455 Teller Road
Thousand Oaks, California 91320
(800) 233-9936
www.corwin.com

SAGE Publications Ltd.
1 Oliver's Yard
55 City Road
London EC1Y 1SP
United Kingdom

SAGE Publications India Pvt. Ltd.
Unit No 323-333, Third Floor, F-Block
International Trade Tower Nehru Place
New Delhi 110 019
India

SAGE Publications Asia-Pacific Pte. Ltd.
18 Cross Street #10-10/11/12
China Square Central
Singapore 048423

Vice President and Editorial Director: Monica Eckman
Senior Acquisitions Editor: Pam Berkman
Content Development Manager: Desirée A. Bartlett
Senior Editorial Assistant: Nyle De Leon
Production Editor: Tori Mirsadjadi
Copy Editor: Pam Schroeder
Typesetter: C&M Digitals (P) Ltd.
Cover Designer: Rose Storey
Marketing Manager: Melissa Duclos

Printed in the United States of America

Library of Congress Cataloging-in-Publication Data

Names: Kirtman, Lyle author

Title: Shaping the future : four leadership pivots for lasting educational impact / Lyle Kirtman.

Description: First edition. | Thousand Oaks, California : Corwin, [2025] | Includes bibliographical references and index.

Identifiers: LCCN 2025003279 | ISBN 9781071949788 paperback | ISBN 9781071987896 epub | ISBN 9781071987902 epub | ISBN 9781071987919 pdf

Subjects: LCSH: Educational leadership | Educational change

Classification: LCC LB2805 .K5237 2025 | DDC 371.2/011—dc23/eng/20250407
LC record available at https://lccn.loc.gov/2025003279

This book is printed on acid-free paper.

25 26 27 28 29 10 9 8 7 6 5 4 3 2 1

CONTENTS

ACKNOWLEDGMENTS

I want to thank Dr. Sybil Burney for working with me on the *Education Week* article that was the basis for this book. Burney stayed with the purpose of this book and supported me even when the content changed midstream. John Pierce has been my thought partner and coach through challenging times. Dr. Michael Fullan has always supported me even when my ideas were way outside of the box.

I thank my wife, Kathleen Keegan, for her personal support; my son, Sean Kirtman, for his patience in teaching me how artificial intelligence can help education; and Beth Saunders for her tireless work on this project, which was well beyond her job description.

Corwin gratefully acknowledges the contributions of the following reviewers:

Helene Alalouf
Instructional and Leadership Coach, Solved Consulting
New York, New York

Peter Dillon
Superintendent, Berkshire Hills Regional School District
Stockbridge, Massachusetts

Louis Lim
Principal, Bur Oak Secondary School
Toronto, Ontario, Canada

Ellen Perconti
Superintendent, Goldendale School District
Goldendale, Washington

Teresa Tung
Secondary School Principal, Hong Kong Academy
Sai Kung, New Territories, Hong Kong SAR

ABOUT THE AUTHOR

Lyle Kirtman has been a leadership development consultant for more than thirty years. As CEO of Future Management Systems Inc. he has worked on developing leaders to increase results for students in 350 school districts in fifteen states. Kirtman's publications are influencing educators nationally and internationally. His books, *Leadership and Teams: The Missing Piece of the Educational Reform Puzzle, Leadership: Key Competencies for Whole System Change* (with Michael Fullan) and *Coherent School Leadership: Forging Clarity from Complexity* (with Michael Fullan), have influenced educational practice throughout the United States.

Kirtman's focus on innovation in education is a key element of his presentations, keynotes, and publications. He helped former Governor Patrick in Massachusetts by chairing the governor's strategic planning task force on innovation in education. Kirtman brings a unique background to his leadership work in education through his consulting experience in the federal government (EPA), health care (Massachusetts General Hospital), universities (Harvard University), and corporate (Cisco Systems) and nonprofit worlds (United Way). He has also worked as a senior administrator in central office for the Boston Public Schools in the organizational development and leadership field for school operations.

Kirtman's field-based research has already made major contributions to the educational leadership arena through his seven competencies for educational leaders, the use of leadership assessments for self-reflection and hiring, and the importance of getting a “C” in compliance to increase focus on results for student achievement.

Kirtman earned a bachelor’s degree in psychology from the State University of New York (SUNY) and a master’s degree in counseling with a concentration in career development from SUNY and Fairfield University, Connecticut.

INTRODUCTION

Why Your Leadership Must Change Now

Education must change, or potentially what we call public education may not exist in the near future. This may seem alarmist, but the signs are clear. Educators are exhausted. The best and brightest are leaving the field at overwhelming levels (Barnum, 2023). The leaders who are supposed to be motivating people to stay are weary and also looking to leave and find a better work-life balance. The public is so divided that every situation gets polarized and escalates to distract everyone from the purpose of why education exists. According to Katherine Norris and Kathryn Wiley (2023), "With low teacher pay, challenging classroom and school conditions, and long-standing underinvestment in education, coupled with the new anti-critical-race-theory and anti-anything-equity movement, teachers are under greater strain. These factors have led to a crisis in our nation's classrooms, unlike anything we have seen in our careers"(p. 3).

The opportunity for positive change requires leaders to pivot to a new mindset to be proactive leaders. The opportunity for courageous leaders is extraordinary. Robert Jokela, executive director of the Crest Collaborative in Massachusetts, visits Finland frequently to reconnect with his family. I asked Bob one day what the Finland educators say about why they are able to succeed when the United States has struggled. What Bob hears is that they do not focus on compliance, assessment, and accountability as much, but they do learn from the U.S. education system. They say that they take many of the great ideas from the United States that have never been implemented but have proven to improve student achievement.

The goal of this book is to place the focus of education back on student achievement. To that end, the reader will find strategies and tools to help them develop a *positive results culture* that will attract a highly skilled and diverse staff. We know that student results are critical. We also know that a positive culture and high morale are needed for staff to feel satisfied that they are making a difference in student and family lives. Now we must combine both to create a positive results culture.

CHARACTERISTICS OF A POSITIVE RESULTS CULTURE

- A feeling of ownership for outcomes by staff and faculty
- Staff and faculty practicing a strong voice in setting goals
- High interdependence and communication
- Intrinsic accountability
- Continuous improvement
- Broad-based leadership, not by title
- Sustainable results
- Less impact by a change at the top
- Celebration of success

This positive results culture will help educators better prepare students for postsecondary education and life. The fact that many of our current educational strategies are not aligned with student achievement is the core disconnect in education. To become aligned we must pivot and shift our leadership. We have defined *four pivots* to make in leadership to build a positive results culture.

Four Pivots in Leadership to Build a Positive Results Culture

THE FOUR PIVOTS

1. Identify a clear North Star that defines what student success looks like.
2. Develop a new approach for hiring, developing, and retaining all staff.
3. Implement a system where employees self-assess their progress toward enabling student success.
4. Establish and commit to high expectations for all students and staff—all the time.

These *four pivots* in leadership mindset and practice will be discussed in Chapters 4, 5, 6, and 7. The reader will learn how to develop actions for change with examples from leaders at all levels. This book will reach beyond our traditional hierarchy of administrative leadership to teachers, support staff, parents, and even students. We truly do need a village to educate a child.

Chapter 1: Our Findings and New Leadership Approach—It's Research Based. The four leadership pivots are based on our research, data, and experience in building leadership capacity in districts nationally. This data can be used to add credibility for these proposed leadership pivots and to inform the strategies for implementation. I conducted a two-year research project in 2011 and 2012 with the support of Pearson Publishing and Association for Supervision and Curriculum Development (ASCD) studying high-performing leaders and their skills and competencies. Using this data we have looked at more than 9,000 leadership assessment reports and found some clear trends for administrators' and teachers' behavior nationally. The most prominent data indicate a lack of focus on student achievement and success.

Chapter 2: Integrate, Don't Separate—A New Leadership Mindset. This chapter will show readers how to change silo mentality and stop the pressure to develop a myriad of stars that distract from the goal of student achievement. Integration will calm your environment and allow for more focus and fewer frenetic reactive actions.

Chapter 3: Finding Your North Star. Education has allowed its North Star to drift. The North Star is the clear definition of what success looks like for students. Education needs to step back and focus on the reason it was created: to provide an academic education, as well as a common political and social philosophy, to all young people regardless of social class.

Chapter 4: Moving From Human Resources to Talent Management—Solving the Workforce Crisis. The number of candidates for almost every position has decreased dramatically. Superintendent searches are lucky to have twenty candidates. Eighty-six percent of school districts reported challenges in hiring teaching positions in 2023-2024 (National Center for Education Statistics, 2023a). Other industries have changed their hiring to look at skills, experience, and who people are; education has not made that change.

Chapter 5: Setting High Expectations for All Students and Staff. If students and staff are treated with respect and coached to success, most people will rise to the occasion. We will outline how we can treat people like professionals. This also means classified staff. All staff can control their own narrative for performance as long as we achieve results.

Chapter 6: Intrinsic Accountability—Student and Staff Agency. We need to demystify this process by allowing those who are being evaluated to have a voice in the process, thus increasing buy-in and accountability. Using an intrinsic accountability system for evaluation will motivate staff to sustainable improvement.

Chapter 7: Call to Action—Rediscover Your North Star. The final chapter will motivate the reader to act by focusing on the four leadership pivots. Most leaders have lost their focus and the ability to ensure that the North Star is a guide through the storms of change. This chapter will bring all aspects of this book into a clear and simplified plan of action. Acting now before it's too late is essential for students, staff, parents, and the community.

Although each chapter covers the different pivots, they are not separate strategies. You will see different topics covered in multiple chapters because they are interconnected with the strategies. We will dive deeply into many aspects of these topics using the different pivot areas and strategies.

Each chapter will provide the following features.

- Learning Intentions: a summary of what the reader will take away from the chapter.
- Statement of the Problem: a description of the problem we are trying to solve (problems that districts and schools are facing nationally)
- Proposed Practical Solutions: solutions the reader can implement to solve the problems districts face
- Suggested Steps and Strategies: how to begin and implement the solutions
- Vignettes and Examples: examples of either the problem or solutions of the chapter focus
- Chapter Summary: key takeaways and steps the reader can use right away for real-life problems

... important

As a person who does not come from the pre-k–12 world, I have been informed by my observations, data, research, and experience that have resulted in conclusions that may be different from those in the education field. I believe in the importance of education and respect people who have chosen that path for their life's work. I know educators are frustrated with outsiders criticizing education. I have a different path. I chose to work within education based on my personal values of commitment to students and families as the basis for positive change in society. What is different in this book is that I am speaking from both theory and practice. I have worked side by side with a state commissioner, superintendents, central office leaders, teachers, parents, support staff, and educational partners in 500 school districts and 1,000 schools. I provide both an outsider and insider viewpoint developed through playing a direct role in implementation with districts across our country. I have additional experience in business, health care, government, and the nonprofit world that I integrate into my work and research.

Other people have discovered many of the same issues based on experience and expertise. However, this book will provide a framework with specific examples of how to be successful that you will not see in other leadership books. As Michael Fullan (2023) has said, often I focus on practice and am informed by the theory. The outsider-insider viewpoint allows me to see the whole system from the student to the policymakers. This book will help the readers align their day-to-day work to student achievement and stay the course without being distracted by all the noise.

1

OUR FINDINGS AND NEW LEADERSHIP APPROACH—IT'S RESEARCH BASED

Learning Intentions

1. Review the data, research, and findings that support the reasoning for why leadership needs to pivot in education.
2. Understand and begin to apply the Seven Competencies for High-Performing Leaders.
3. Consider the Four Pivots education needs to undertake.

The Context of Why We Need to Pivot

The purpose of our research was to determine if our data and experience on leadership would be supported with evidence. Our intention was to deepen the leadership development conversations and help inform educators on how to focus their practice to maximize student results.

Following is the description of the methodology of how the research was conducted and how it can be used in leadership development work in districts. Figure 1.1 illustrates the process Future Management Systems (FMS) and Pearson went through to align the Workplace Personality Inventory (WPI) and my Seven Competences for High-Performing Leaders.

1.1 The Description and Methodology of the Future Management Systems/Pearson Research Study

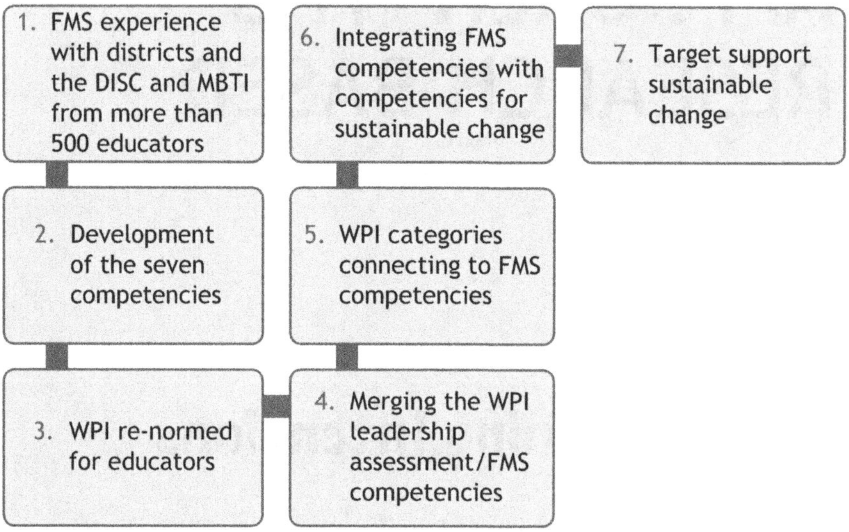

In 2011 I developed the Seven Competencies of High-Performance Leaders based on a combination of my experience working with and coaching leaders in more than 700 school districts and 1,000 schools, the DiSC inventory, and a nationwide Myers Briggs Type Indicator (MBTI) database on education leaders. I believe that "high-performance education leaders have a range of leadership skills, competencies, and personal attributes. Although the core service in education is instruction for students, the leader's role is to ensure that the highest quality of service is provided" (Kirtman, 2014). I believe that "our most successful leaders in education are results oriented" (Kirtman 2014).

Based on the Seven Competencies of High-Performance Leaders, Pearson and TalentLens wanted to conduct a study to re-norm the WPI, a self-assessment inventory, for school principals and to correlate the WPI traits to the Seven Competencies of High-Performance

Leaders. To do this study, TalentLens reviewed WPI results from 200 principals. The superintendents of the participating districts rated the principals using a Likert scale on their effectiveness (school success) and rated the principals' leadership using the subsets of the Seven Competencies (see "Seven Competencies for High-Performing Leaders"). The principals then all took the WPI. As hypothesized, the WPI scales significantly predicted a number of competencies that had been identified as important for successful performance as a principal.

The WPI is a highly effective, valid, and reliable tool. The WPI traits correspond with the workstyle job requirements listed in the ONET* system for the Department of Labor. Using the results of the WPI and the superintendents' ratings of each principal on the Seven Competencies, TalentLens and I drew correlations between the Seven Competencies and the WPI traits. We then mapped the traits to the competencies. Additionally, the results of the study provided a range of scores desirable in school leadership, which are outlined later in the chapter with the trait definitions. These scores are not good or bad but rather reflective of behavior at work. Finally, we drew themes from the study, which resulted in significant research findings (see "Key Findings From Our Research"). Subsequently, our database has expanded to more than 9,000 WPIs from superintendents, central office administrators, principals, and more 2,000 teachers. The original results of the research have held true through the expansion to other groups beyond principals.

Since this research, we have been working on redefining results for students through the development of a clear North Star, which combines standardized tests (hard skills) and soft skills through the process of developing a portrait of a graduate. This new concept of developing a North Star is defined and outlined in Chapter 3.

You can find the description of the research tool and the data from the study in Appendix F. It was my opinion that it was important to explain the research findings and lessons learned from the data to the reader without the complications of understanding leadership assessments. The specific results in Appendix F will be helpful for people who are familiar with these leadership assessments or are interested in pursuing their use in their district.

SEVEN COMPETENCIES FOR HIGH-PERFORMING LEADERS

A High Performing Leader . . .

1. Challenges the Status Quo
   - ✓ Delegates compliance tasks to other staff
   - ✓ Challenges common practices and traditions if they are blocking improvements
   - ✓ Is willing to take risks
   - ✓ Looks for innovations to get results
   - ✓ Does not let rules and regulations block results and slow action
2. Builds Trust Through Clear Communications and Expectations
   - ✓ Is direct and honest about performance expectations
   - ✓ Follows through with actions on all commitments
   - ✓ Makes sure there is a clear understanding based on written and verbal communications
   - ✓ Is comfortable dealing with conflict
3. Creates a Commonly Owned Plan for Success
   - ✓ Creates written plans with input from stakeholders
   - ✓ Ensures that people buy into the plan
   - ✓ Monitors implementation of the plan
   - ✓ Adjusts the plan based on new data, and communicates changes clearly
   - ✓ Develops clear measurement for each goal in the plan
   - ✓ Creates short- and long-term plans
4. Focuses on Team Over Self
   - ✓ Hires the best people for the team
   - ✓ Commits to the ongoing development of a high-performance leadership team

- ✓ Builds a team environment
- ✓ Seeks critical feedback
- ✓ Empowers staff to make decisions and get results
- ✓ Supports the professional development of all staff

5. Has a High Sense of Urgency for Change and Sustainable Results in Improving Student Achievement

    - ✓ Moves initiatives ahead quickly
    - ✓ Can be decisive
    - ✓ Uses instructional data to support needed change
    - ✓ Builds systemic strategies to insure sustainability of change
    - ✓ Sets a clear direction for the organization
    - ✓ Deals with and manages change effectively

6. Commits to Continuous Improvement for Self and the Organization

    - ✓ High sense of curiosity for new ways to get results
    - ✓ Is willing to change current practices for themselves and others
    - ✓ Listens to all team members to change practices to obtain results
    - ✓ Takes responsibility for their own actions—no excuses
    - ✓ Has a strong self-management and self-reflection skills

7. Builds External Networks and Partnerships

    - ✓ Sees their role as a leader on a broad base manner outside the work environment and community walls
    - ✓ Understands their role as being a part of a variety of external networks for change and improvement
    - ✓ Has a strong ability to engage people inside and outside in two-way partnerships
    - ✓ Uses technology to expand and manage a network of resource people

Prior to the COVID-19 pandemic, education had faced the need for change based on the challenges of educating students in a quickly evolving world. However, the pandemic has put a spotlight on the need to change to improve student achievement. Additionally, the current workforce crisis has created ongoing concerns regarding student achievement, and a volatile political environment has increased the pressure to change quickly. A district problem that took months to escalate in the past can move to crisis level in days or even hours. As one teacher told us, "The pandemic put the change process on steroids!"

Challenges the Status Quo (Competency 1) was important pre-pandemic; now it is a necessity. Our current education system has maintained strategies and practices that do not work in today's world. "Why has the 200-year-old current system in Western societies not transformed when the majority of people have known for at least 50 years that it does not work?" (Fullan, 2023, p 2). People know that we need to change our education system but fear the criticism they may receive from all sides when they try. My leadership research provides objective data to help us understand what needs to change, why we tend to maintain the status quo, and information on how we can move forward.

KEY FINDINGS FROM OUR RESEARCH

- District and school leaders need leadership skills and competencies beyond instructional leadership.
- Top-down leaders do not create sustainable change.
- Most leaders are cautious and don't have a high sense of urgency for student achievement.
- External networking and partnerships increase results.
- Motivating staff gets better results than the traditional evaluation process.
- Stress and defensiveness from data and critical feedback decrease positive results and improvement.
- Leaders who are overly concerned with others are less able to give feedback and often get lower results.
- Focusing on compliance and rule following decreases positive results.

My book with Michael Fullan, *Leadership: Key Competencies for Whole System Change* (Kirtman & Fullan, 2017), provides more depth on the Seven Competencies. In addition, my second book with Fullan (Fullan

& Kirtman, 2019) connects the Seven Competencies to his framework for creating coherent districts and schools.

The Pearson/TalentLens study provides data on leadership for administrators and teachers and the traits that are most critical for thriving in today's educational environment. The data also show how some traits that leaders have are not conducive to success.

Teachers prioritize the work that their principal and the district leadership deems must be completed. The data show that most teachers focus on completing those tasks rather than doing what they believe is best for students. To succeed the teacher who is closest to the student needs to focus on student learning, not task completion and compliance. For example, if a teacher is asked to use a new lesson plan because the central office thinks it is better, a high-performing teacher may resist because they believe the students are learning with the current lesson plan, especially if the reason for the change is not clear. Conversely, a teacher who is task oriented and compliance driven will do what they are told and follow the directive from central office and the principal. This task orientation can be a problem when student achievement does not improve. The teacher may not feel responsible because they did what they were told to do. This can result in a teacher believing that it is the principal's job to improve student achievement, not theirs.

Another key point derived from the data is that the superintendents are focused on behaviors that relate to achieving results. These behaviors show results orientation and a high sense of urgency (Competency 5). The superintendent may also use other leadership traits such as innovation, analytical behaviors on how data can help focus on improving results, independence, and persistence. However, their leadership teams, comprising central office leaders and principals, are generally more focused on implementing and not leading improvement efforts. Therefore, the traits of this team may be lower in the leadership traits exhibited by the superintendent.

This major gap between many superintendents and the central office and school leadership has several implications. The superintendent can lead change but must encourage their leadership teams, including teachers, to not only implement goals and initiatives but be partners in the leadership efforts. Closing this gap will enhance the change and improvement effort and create more sustainable change (Competency 5).

The research also confirmed our concern about educator stress, especially teachers. Most educators' results indicated a high level of stress and a potential to be defensive when sharing data on improvement strategies. Our study showed that defensive behavior, and lack of focus on data, is directly related to stress along with the pressure of completing an overwhelming number of disparate tasks. This teacher stress can affect the students, and we will reference data confirming this result from a leadership assessment called Indigo, which can be completed by students and adults (see Chapter 5).

Stress can also be related to a lack of self-control behaviors by several leaders and especially teachers. This lack of self-control manifests itself in frustration and resistance to change. The use of data to prove the importance of change tends to increase the defensiveness of educators in most cases. The ability to discuss how changes will improve results and address teacher concerns is more effective than showing data on students' low performance and failure. When I discuss data, I use the phrase *data informed* rather than *data driven* to decrease defensiveness. *Data informed* shows more respect and value for the teacher's viewpoint and brings them into the conversation. *Data driven* highlights an external factor that distances a teacher from the data you are trying to use to get their attention and commit to change.

Innovation is important in today's world. We can't solve today's challenges with yesterday's solutions. We also need to help students develop their innovation skills for the workplace. Innovation is a relatively strong trait for administrators and teachers. However, the pressure on compliance and rules decreases innovation. Our data show how innovative people can become frustrated and blocked from pursuing new ideas for fear that they will find themselves in trouble if they do not follow the rules. Some innovative people can decrease their initiative over time because they meet resistance and are discouraged from trying to challenge the status quo. We have also found that educators can become less flexible because of the focus on compliance. This lack of flexibility can have an adverse effect and result in less innovative and affect a teacher's openness to change. Concerns about stifling innovation show up in our disaggregated data on race and gender. Leaders of color tend to have a desire to be innovative but show a decrease in initiative from feeling a lack of support.

One more result from our research is that caring and concern for others, which tends to motivate many to become teachers and administrators, has become a strength *and* a weakness. Caring for students and colleagues is important. However, caring (i.e., avoiding hurt feelings) can prevent an educator's willingness to be open and honest with others. The ability to be direct with caring is important. Educators need to be direct and identify issues early to make sure that their and their colleagues' work and behaviors are focused on results. As some people say, clear is kind, and this is a theme that we will refer to in future chapters.

The implications of the data on educational leaders will be woven into each chapter. The data have also been disaggregated for race, gender, and age, which will be referenced in Chapter 4 on talent management.

SETTING A GOAL TO STRATEGICALLY IMPROVE ACHIEVEMENT SCORE

Danielle Hinkle, a member of the school leadership team who coaches and supervises principals in Modesto School District in California, has been working on increasing her achievement score for two years. She was an excellent member of several teams in student support services and was known for her ability to get tasks done on time. Everyone wanted Danielle on their team. Her achievement score, which reflects results orientation, was low, and her leadership score was also low when she took the WPI for the first time. After gaining self-awareness of her personality traits and their impact on her work performance, she set a clear goal to improve her achievement score. She recognized the need to shift her focus from detailed, task-oriented project management to addressing broader challenges and solutions. This meant starting with focusing on the desired outcomes and strategically determining the steps to achieve them, allowing her to align her work more effectively with high-impact results. By adopting a strategic, outcome-focused approach, she has seen significant improvements in the results of her work and the work of the school leadership team. This shift has enhanced her project execution, ensuring initiatives align more closely with the district's strategic goals. The impact on student achievement has been evident through more cohesive program implementations, streamlined processes, and the fostering of a learning environment that prioritizes both academic rigor and student engagement. These improvements have translated to more targeted support her principals and her colleagues and, ultimately, a more effective

(Continued)

(Continued)

pathway for student success. The outcome-driven mindset has reinforced alignment between district strategies and measurable student outcomes, creating a more unified and impactful educational experience.

Detailed student data with improvements:

- Increased graduation rates
- Decreased dropout rates
- Successful implementation of a college and career readiness platform designed to support students in a greater level of career awareness and how high school course plans can support postsecondary goals for college and career

As part of our leadership development work, we disaggregated the WPI data based on race, gender, and age. I found several themes in our leadership development work. There will be some references to these themes throughout the chapters of this book. This data have been reviewed by the Pearson research team and are aligned with our research study. Although the data have not been peer reviewed or published, they have been integrated into the work with school districts nationally. The following are some of the most applicable themes that have implications for how leaders need to pivot their leadership approach:

1. Young leaders (ages 25–30) have high focus on results, which decreases as they get older and gain more experience. One cause may be that culture in education drives leaders to be more focused on tasks over results over time.
2. Leaders of color have high scores in many of the traits we are looking for to lead and manage in today's educational environment. These include high scores in results orientation, analytical thinking, innovation, and persistence.
3. Leaders of color tend to be able to manage stress relatively well and are open to critical feedback on how to improve.
4. Leaders of color, although having several strong leadership behaviors, tend to have low initiative. The culture in education seems to frustrate leaders of color, and they tend to decrease their initiative over time.

5. Women have high concern for others. They also have low stress tolerance and can struggle with hearing critical feedback if it is not presented constructively.

While I will be expressing my opinion based on extensive experience, the data support these thoughts and recommendations.

How This Research Informed the Four Pivots

Pivot 1—The North Star: The data show a lack of focus and understanding of what the outcomes are for students. This confusion over outcomes can be an aspect of why educators are more task oriented than results driven.

Pivot 2—The Movement to Talent Management: The workforce crisis has many causes. One is that the skills and competencies of the past do not serve us as well in today's educational environment. We must define our North Star and recruit, develop, and retain a workforce that has the skills for now and the future (not the past).

Pivot 3—High Expectations: This pivot is informed by our data that show how compliance, task focus, and rules have prevented educators' ability to focus on results for students. The pressures of today to implement separate initiatives not tied to a clear measurement of success has resulted in lowering our standards for staff and students. Even initiatives such as social emotional learning (SEL) and diversity, equity, and inclusion DEI), which are important to understanding who our students are and what challenges they face, can result in lowering standards because they are not integrated into the high expectations of all students.

Pivot 4—Intrinsic Evaluation: This pivot is directly informed by our data. The stress and frustration of a more top-down system of driving change can be demotivating to the educators we need to lead. Our understanding that there is no data that extrinsic evaluation improves performance is a driving force to focus on driving a teacher's improvement to the understanding of the results we want to achieve.

The four pivots are grounded in the data and research and offer a package of pivots that will broaden student achievement efforts of all educators and reduce the stress that is resulting in the best people leaving education.

As one union leader said to me, "I can get behind your pivots because you are helping us focus and simplify our work."

Proposed Use of the Data

SHIFTING YOUR DISTRICT'S WORK

1. Each staff member must learn how to define results for themselves and the district first before completing tasks. The result is never the task; the task, if done correctly, gets you to the result. This connection between task and results is effective management and argues for more training and coaching on management to improve implementation. Kate Dias, president of the state teacher's union in Connecticut, agrees that we need to increase the management skills for educators.

2. Increase persistence on completing goals, not a list of tasks—lack of persistence is an indicator of stress because educators are constantly distracted by less important tasks that are not connected to results for students.

3. Distribute leadership throughout your district; don't simply delegate tasks. There is a need to raise the leadership of all staff, not only formal leaders.

4. Coach educators on developing a new set of skills and behaviors with a focus on achievement, persistence, leadership, innovation, analytical thinking, and flexibility.

5. Address the stress and self-control data by giving all staff a voice. We need our educators to be owners, not renters.

6. Coach and train all staff to have regular, direct conversations—people who score too high on concern for others may not give constructive feedback. When cooperation and concern for others traits on the WPI are too high, this indicates a reluctance to give clear, actionable feedback.

7. Because analytical behavior is low for most educators, switch from *data-driven* to *data-informed* in meetings. When a teacher who scores low in analytical hears *data-driven,* they can believe that the data are more important than they are. The *phrase data-informed* opens the conversation to acknowledge what the teacher believes is working or not working in their classroom.

Their voice is valued, and then the shift to how data can provide another viewpoint to inform their practice will be perceived as less combative or punitive. Analytical scores need to be higher but not too high, or people can become paralyzed from action for fear of making a mistake.

8. Build the capacity of instructional coaches to lead change in both content and organizational behavior for teachers to improve student achievement. I was part of a research study into the correlation between effective instructional coaches and WPI scores. This study found a positive correlation between high scores on the traits of achievement, self-control, and concern for others to effective coaching for student achievement. The most effective coaches are those who can define a clear result, follow a rigorous process for defining what is getting in the way. and provide direct, actionable feedback to teachers on improving their practice (Kutz et al., 2020).

9. Increase time and support for networking to improve social scores. Coach people to do more in person, on the phone, or virtual face-to-face communication, not only texts and emails. Texts and emails are better to provide information and get quick answers, not solve problems.

APPLY DATA AND RESEARCH

Leadership teams at the district and school levels need to discuss the findings provided in this chapter and assess their strengths and areas for improvement. This can be done by completing the self-assessment tool on the Seven Competencies in Appendix A. Leadership assessments, such as the WPI, can also be helpful in this process.

1. Each individual and team should identify one or two strengths and one or two traits for improvement or development based on the WPI data provided in this chapter.

2. After reflecting on Kirtman's Seven Competencies, ask each member of a district or school leadership team to complete the self-assessment in Appendix A and identify their strengths and weaknesses in each of the Seven Competencies. Then ask everyone to identify one competency that they want to develop over the course of the academic year (Appendix E). Have everyone come up with a plan for how to develop their competency of focus, and then have the team meet and share their plans with each other.

CHAPTER SUMMARY

The data and research outlined in this chapter provide a foundation and a rationale for pivoting your leadership. Educational leaders and teachers have grown frustrated with the environment. I have outlined what has caused this decline and the subsequent frustration and stress that are causing educators to leave the field they were so passionate to join. The data explain how the lack of results focus is a core factor in the decline. The leadership directives coming from above without the genuine commitment to develop leadership capacity for all educators has resulted in a feeling of helplessness. The compliance requirements have become overwhelming and prevented educators from focusing on the students' learning. The hope is that the inherent innovation that still exists in our educators can be rekindled and the clarity of the North Star and the other leadership pivots can bring back the reason people enter the educational field. Use these conclusions from our research to gain the courage to shift now and stop the decline.

CHAPTER TAKEAWAYS

- It is important to have discussions on the data trends and themes from the research about adult leaders and students and faculty.
- Teachers need to have training and coaching on how to connect better with their students to engage them in learning.
- Begin to discuss the Four Pivots for leadership and the data that support the new leadership approach.
- Talk to teachers and students about how the educational process connects to their needs and lives.
- Decrease the focus on compliance and tasks, and tie all your work to outcomes for students.

QUESTIONS FOR REFLECTION

1. Do the data trends for leaders, faculty, and students resonate with you? Why or why not?
2. How can you engage in connecting with students and staff to help them focus on results?
3. Are there one or two themes that you believe are relevant to your district, school or a specific class? Why?
4. Have an honest conversation with a colleague about why the disconnect among administrators, teachers, and students occurs in your district.
5. How can you explore this data without feeling defensive or attacked for true learning and insights?

2

INTEGRATE, DON'T SEPARATE

A New Leadership Mindset

Learning Intentions

1. Understand integrative thinking as a key skill for leadership.
2. Use the integrative thinking process to ease the stress of educators.
3. Learn how integrative thinking can free up time for everyone, get better results for students, and provide opportunities for work-life balance.
4. Apply integrative thinking to decrease political tensions in districts.

What Is the Problem We Are Trying to Solve?

Often the federal and state departments of education (DOEs) develop policies and initiatives to help school systems without input from educators. The way the educational system and policy development process works is that the federal and state legislature and their DOEs keep most initiatives separate to meet the specific needs of individuals and groups. There is minimal effort or incentive for the DOEs to integrate or connect initiatives to student success.

These separate initiatives are often well intended but do not consider the effect on districts and schools that are charged with implementation. District leaders try to implement these separate initiatives and find themselves constantly distracted by sudden changes and often unfunded mandates. These distractions are passed on to the schools and prevent principals and teachers from focusing on student achievement.

RESULTS FOR STUDENTS HAPPEN VERTICALLY (K-12), NOT HORIZONTALLY

A Texas superintendent had two requests for plans for improvement from the state DOE, an elementary plan and a secondary plan. Because he had little time to meet these requests, he produced a district plan that addressed student outcomes from pre-K to graduation. He was told by the state that the plans needed to be separate. He was frustrated that his plan, driven by the outcomes at graduation and back-planned to pre-K, was not valued. The superintendent sent in two plans to the state but used the whole district plan. This is an example of the state's failure to integrate and focus on student results.

Because the system will likely never change, what can educational leaders, who find themselves constantly reacting to legislation or the initiative du jour, do? Leaders will need to fundamentally change their leadership mindset to practice this motto: Integrate, don't separate.

Superintendents, principals, and teacher associations always complain to the state DOE about these disparate and often unfunded mandates and how they are causing problems in their districts. Unfortunately, these mandates come with compliance requirements and often have grants for funding that perpetuate their implementation in silos. Each initiative that may become legislation is rarely connected to any common goals for student success.

The assumption by most state DOEs is that educators do not have the expertise to properly develop programs to educate students. Teachers and unions are often seen as blocking new ideas and best practices. Expert educational consultants on reading, math, science, social emotional learning (SEL), equity, and a myriad of other areas receive statewide contracts to impart their knowledge to teachers. The unions and teachers often object to this approach. Because teachers have little input into these efforts, and the contracts are driven by outside consultants, teachers have minimal control with no voice on how programs are implemented.

We have found that teachers are much more open to learning if they are treated as professionals and can integrate new learning and practice into their teaching:

> While many voice support for teachers, there are many policies and realities of being a teacher that do not demonstrate our respect for the expertise, commitment, and creativity that it takes to meet the needs of all students every day. Lifting up our teachers and treating them as professionals are critical to continuing to recruit and retain excellent teachers in our schools. (Wolf, 2021)

Additionally, Robert Bruno (2018), in the *Harvard Business Review* said, "Teachers are seeing their own experience be devalued by policymakers and other officials with little experience in the education field, and it's not improving the education of their students. In other words, and as others have noted, teachers are balking at the erosion of their status as professionals." A superintendent in Texas stated that teachers are treated with "disdain" in today's educational environment. One teacher said that if they object to a new program, they are insubordinate, and if they agree and students do not improve, policymakers conclude that they do not know what they are doing. A successful approach would be to treat teachers as professionals with high expectations. We will provide more depth on this in Chapters 5 and 6.

Silo initiatives in education are so numerous that it is hard to make a complete list, but here are some categories:

- Dyslexia legislation
- The science of reading
- Math programs
- Science programs

- SEL
- Diversity, equity, and inclusion (DEI)
- School councils
- Wellness programs
- Standardized tests
- Nutrition programs

Too often school boards and superintendents add their initiatives to the long list from the state and federal government. It is getting so bad that the stress tolerance of teachers is reaching serious lows on the Workplace Personality Inventory (WPI). A score for a successful leader is 50 and above, and teachers have been measured as a median 16, meaning that the stress tolerance level is so low and the feeling of defensiveness against change is so high that teachers are burning out or leaving the profession at unsustainable levels. Unfortunately, administrators are not much better at managing stress, with a median score of 33 on stress tolerance. This means that their energy to help teachers is so low that the problem is getting much worse.

Dr. Ebony Green, a former DEI leader and author of the book *Acts of Liberation*, has described an example of this silo mentality in education initiatives:

DEI MUST BE PART OF EVERYONE'S WORK

During my tenure as a DEI executive, I encountered numerous obstacles that, in many ways, seemed to challenge the core objectives of my role. One notable hurdle was the sense of isolation that can accompany this position. Instead of being part of a collaborative team, I often worked within a specific division or department, which limited opportunities for cross-functional collaboration.

This setup placed the significant responsibility of addressing systemic inequities primarily on one area, which highlighted the importance of teamwork in tackling these complex challenges. It became evident that DEI initiatives cannot thrive in isolation; they require integration across all facets of an organization or school system. True progress demands that DEI principles be interwoven into the fabric of every department, each with its tailored focus reflecting its unique function. For example, in Human Resources, a DEI objective might focus on enhancing the recruitment and retention of underrepresented groups, while in Curriculum and Instruction, the emphasis could shift to developing equity-driven educational goals and supports. To achieve equitable outcomes, it's essential to have a cohesive plan that aligns the efforts of each department and ensures we're working towards a shared vision.

Another pervasive challenge was the gap between awareness and action. While we could facilitate training sessions aimed at broadening understanding and deepening the DEI knowledge of colleagues, these efforts often hit a wall when it came to tangible implementation and accountability. For example, despite conducting comprehensive diversity, equity, and inclusion workshops, there is no clear mechanism to track how these insights translated into real changes in classroom dynamics or organizational culture. This disconnect meant that, despite significant efforts to enrich our collective understanding and commitment to DEI, the tangible impact on our educational environments and the lived experiences of those we aimed to support remained elusive.

These experiences underscored a critical lesson: The journey towards equity is not just about education and awareness but requires a systemic transformation that embeds accountability and action into the very heart of our institutions.

How do we reverse these trends? First, we need to think differently and change our mindset. To stop this spiralling problem, the concept of integrative thinking must become the focus for all leadership and teachers. In this chapter we propose developing a new integrative thinking mindset, putting integrative thinking into practice and integrating DEI and SEL into academics.

[illegible]

Integrative thinking is the ability to keep two or more concepts, ideas, or competing issues in your head at one time. The integrative thinker resists the temptation to choose one option to proceed. Instead, they listen to all viewpoints and determine an approach that integrates the key ideas into one strategy. A simple way to say this is one plus one is not always two; it may be three. Integration is not compromised. The new integrated solution combines the best of all viewpoints into a goal or strategy that best meets the needs of the students. Using this method no one wins, and no one loses.

Some readers may want to know if integrative thinking is the same as systems thinking. Both approaches are important for educators to learn to become result oriented.

INTEGRATIVE THINKING IN EDUCATION

- **Definition:** Integrative thinking involves considering multiple, often conflicting, perspectives and synthesizing them to create a new solution that incorporates elements of each. It's about creatively resolving tensions between opposing ideas.
- **Application:** In education, integrative thinking can help administrators, teachers, and students approach conflicting goals, such as balancing student achievement with well-being. For example, an integrative thinker might merge traditional teaching with progressive methods aiming to maximize both engagement and rigor.

SYSTEMS THINKING IN EDUCATION

- **Definition:** Systems thinking focuses on understanding how different parts of a system interact to create outcomes. It involves recognizing interdependencies and feedback loops within a whole system.
- **Application:** In education, systems thinking is particularly useful in analyzing how elements like curriculum design, school culture, policies, and community factors influence each other. For instance, an educator might analyze how family engagement, classroom management, and curriculum changes interact and affect student achievement.

The following vignette concerns a leader, Madeline Smola, who practiced integrative thinking in her job when she felt hopelessly paralyzed and overworked. The vignette has been organized according to Roger Martin's (2007) four steps of integrative thinking.

COMPLIANCE OR SUCCESS—WE CAN DO BOTH!

Step 1: Identify key factors

A grant writer, in a rural district in the Northeast, Madeline Smola, was trying to raise money for innovation. An available state grant had a prescribed set of steps to complete; it was designed to establish an innovative pathway focused on bio-medical opportunities. The grant listed the people who should have input and the pathways the state believed were viable. The state prescribed the questions to ask relevant partners in the community they designated. It did not ask anything about student achievement. Was the purpose of the grant to follow the state plan or to increase the innovative skills and opportunities for students and teachers?

Smola practiced integrative thinking by staying focused on her outcomes for students while integrating state compliance into a strategy that would develop the skills for students to be successful. She pivoted to focus on the North Star and establish high expectations while meeting compliance requirements. The state's compliance requirements did not focus on the outcome and in fact could have limited the opportunity to provide great career choices for students.

Step 2: Analyze causality

This step changed the perspective of the grant writer to focus on results and look for opportunities to find potential partners for the district. Could the grant writer's first focus be "success for students in an open and innovative manner"? Could this open process work even though the state was proposing a closed and structured process?

Step 3: Envision the decision's overall structure

Holding both an open-ended process for innovation at the same time holding the state's closed process without choosing one over the other can be difficult. At first the grant writer was nervous that she would fail with this approach. However, she held the potential competing thoughts that the grant was not the outcome but rather a learning opportunity for students that could become sustainable in her district, which had minimal funds for innovation.

Step 4: Achieve resolution

The grant writer opened herself to be free of the grant restrictions and broadened her network of potential partners without asking only the prescribed state questions. This resulted in finding new partners, such as veterinarians, who were not on the state's list.

She also found ways to engage principals and teachers in the possibilities and benefits of the program, which increased the internal buy-in.

(Continued)

(Continued)

Now she could build a program that the district would be proud of supporting. The tension of the state grant was also resolved, the grant writer provided the information needed within the grant and show how her district could move beyond the grant's goals to greater success for more students.

The result was the district received the grant and has obtained follow-up funds for their expanded program. The result for our grant writer is that her vision and courage to be an integrated thinker resulted in a broader title of development director, and now she is an assistant superintendent. In addition, she obtained a grant for teacher leadership with a focus on teaching integrative thinking.

Martin (2007) brought everything together when he surmised: "A leader who embraces holistic rather than segmented thinking can creatively resolve the tensions that launched the decision-making process." Many of today's educational issues have major tensions that are ripe for integrated thinking to move problems to opportunities. These problems, if allowed to persist, lead to an unfocused learning environment for students and teachers. Unfortunately, when you are in the middle of chaos, it's difficult to see your way out. That's when you have to pull yourself out of the situation long enough to regroup your priorities, rethink your goals, refocus on your vision, and sometimes redefine your ultimate mission. Our political environment today is ripe for integrative thinking to deal with the polarizing tensions in every community. Instead of taking a political side, integrative thinking focuses on goals and integrates the different viewpoints into a solution. For example, the controversy surrounding critical race theory can be mitigated by teaching all history and not naming the program or topic.

In addition to the four steps, Martin (2007) has also provided a chart (see Figure 2.1) that contrasts conventional thinking with integrative thinking. This comparison further clarifies that conventional thinkers seek almost simple or even status quo solutions. This may even be called a Band-Aid type of remedy that offers only temporary solutions, whereas integrative thinkers involve themselves in problem-solving that is more complex and results in solutions that are creative and innovative. Therein lies the key to resolving the tension within the process, s process that demands patience, vulnerability, and trust. Martin (2007) has concluded: "Integrative thinking generates options and new solutions. It creates a sense of limitless possibility."

2.1 The Four Steps of Integrative Thinking

Steps	Conventional Thinking	Integrative Thinking
Step 1: Identify key factors	Considers only relevant factors while weighing options	Seeks less obvious but potentially more relevant considerations
Step 2: Analyze causality	Considers one-way, linear relationships between factors	Considers multidirectional relationships
Step 3: Envision the decision's overall structure	Breaks a problem into pieces, and work on them separately	Sees a problem as a whole, examining how its various aspects affect one another
Step 4: Achieve resolution	Makes either-or choices	Refuses to accept conventional options

Source: Martin (2007)

[illegible] into Practice

Integrative thinking is a problem-solving approach that involves integrating multiple perspectives to develop creative and innovative solutions. Expanding on Martin's four steps, I have outlined six steps.

STEPS FOR IMPLEMENTING INTEGRATIVE THINKING

Step 1: Articulate the Problem

- Identify the Challenge: Clearly define the problem or decision you are facing.
- Frame the Problem: Understand the context and scope of the issue.

Step 2: Seek Multiple Perspectives

- Gather Diverse Views: Engage with a variety of stakeholders to understand different perspectives.

(Continued)

(Continued)

- Consider Opposing Ideas: Deliberately seek out and consider ideas that conflict with each other.

Step 3: Generate Options

- Brainstorm Solutions: Develop a wide range of possible solutions without immediate judgment.
- Explore Extremes: Consider extreme or unconventional solutions to broaden the range of options.

Step 4: Evaluate and Synthesize

- Assess Pros and Cons: Evaluate the advantages and disadvantages of each option.
- Combine Elements: Look for ways to combine elements of different solutions to create a new, integrative solution.
- Develop a Prototype: Create a prototype or model of the integrated solution to test its viability.

Step 5: Test and Refine

- Implement on a Small Scale: Test the integrated solution on a small scale or in a controlled environment.
- Gather Feedback: Collect feedback from stakeholders, and observe the outcomes.
- Refine the Solution: Make adjustments based on feedback and further analysis.

Step 6: Implement and Monitor

- Move Forward on the Solution: Implement the refined solution on a larger scale.
- Monitor Progress: Continuously monitor the implementation to ensure it meets the desired outcomes.
- Adapt as Needed: Be prepared to make further adjustments as new information and feedback becomes available.

Let's review a few key issues in education today that are being approached with a conventional leadership approach. We will outline how to move to integrative thinking to unlock the skills of the leaders we must have now. Issues are becoming polarized with each side hanging onto their position for fear of losing. If we don't use integrative thinking to bring conflicting sides together, no one will win, and everyone will lose—specifically the students.

Leaders who are leading in a conventional way are losing their jobs because of volatility, and quickly escalating issues put them in a defensive position. Any action they take will anger someone. We need to change the mindset for leadership in districts and in schools to integrate these disparate programs that become silos and potential flash points. Integrating these programs will take courage, focus, and commitment. The amount of time and effort it takes to work on every issue separately is completely burning out educators. What will integration do? The number of committees, separate plans, and reports will dramatically reduce. One of the biggest complaints we hear is that educators are too busy running from meeting to meeting, so they can't get the work done. Integration will free up time to put into the development of more effective strategies to educate our children! We can have more effective and efficient plans and strategies for success without introducing new initiatives.

PROBLEMS ARISING WHEN INITIATIVES ARE NOT INTEGRATED

Fragmentation: Without integration, initiatives may exist in silos, leading to disjointed efforts and a lack of coherence in the educational system.

Inefficiency: Schools and educational institutions may duplicate efforts or resources when initiatives are not integrated, leading to wasted time and money.

Confusion: Teachers, students, and other stakeholders may become confused or overwhelmed by conflicting or inconsistent messages and practices.

Lack of alignment: When initiatives are not integrated, they may not align with the overall goals and objectives of the educational institution, leading to a lack of progress toward desired outcomes.

Missed opportunities: Not integrating initiatives can result in missed opportunities for innovation, collaboration, and improvement in the educational system.

Limited impact: Each initiative may have a limited impact on its own, but when integrated, they can have a more significant and lasting impact on student learning outcomes.

Resistance to change: Without integration, stakeholders may be more resistant to change because they may not see the value or relevance of new initiatives to their current practices.

Failure to meet goals: Ultimately, not integrating initiatives can hinder the ability of educational institutions to meet their goals and objectives for student learning and success.

Most districts would agree that they have many of the problems described here. The shift to integrated thinking will minimize the problems and provide more time and energy to work on high-impact, high-results strategies.

SCIENCE OF READING—AN EXAMPLE OF CONVENTIONAL THINKING VERSUS INTEGRATIVE THINKING

One example in education that could be a game changer in improving student achievement is the science of reading. Brain research is compelling, and the benefits to all students are indisputable. There are national and state legislation and programs on how the teaching of reading must change to improve literacy for all students. However, the legislation, programs, coaching, and grants are in separate silos. Districts are told that they have to have science of reading committees, curriculum, plans, coaches, and grants. They are being told what programs they must adopt. In one state they have to apply for waivers from the DOE to use different programs regardless of their results for all students.

We have lost our focus on learning and student achievement. The fight is not about student success; it is about adult issues and their concern for power and control. Many states believe they have the power to make needed changes and are directing districts to use certain programs. Mandating change is conventional thinking and has few prospects of gaining sustainable change. Change driven by the district with outside consultation and perspective is more likely to result in sustainable success. In an *EdWeek* article describing state legislation regarding the science of reading Schwarts (2022) stated, "The researchers found that while most measures mandate an evidence-based approach to reading instruction, few define exactly what that means. And though the majority require teacher professional learning and preservice training, most don't offer the implementation support needed to change school systems on a broad scale." She further stated,

> For many schools, these laws mandate a wholesale change in how reading is taught, requiring new methods, new curriculum materials, new tests, and new ways of using time during the school day. Putting all these changes into

> practice, and making sure they work together, requires leadership, planning, and continuous support, and implementation, science experts have said. (Schwartz, 2022)

In addition, large numbers of district educators are being left out of any decision-making and object to the prescribed programs. The conventional thinkers feel they have to choose a side in this battle.

The integrative thinker steps back and refocuses. Literacy coaches in some states are working with districts on how to implement the legislation or initiative. A reading coach who is an integrative thinker would say that the result is student learning and success in postsecondary education and in life; the science of reading as foundational, not the focus. The integrative leader understands that literacy is a foundation for all learning. Reading connects to math and science. Instead of a separate committee, reading should be integrated into a system-wide strategy of learning. The work would involve one committee or team on learning with reading, math, and science following the same path. This integrated approach should be led by the leadership teams in each school.

HIGH SCHOOLS DO NOT NEED TO TEACH READING

Using Roger Martin's four steps in integrative thinking, a district leader improved student achievement.

Step 1: Identify key factors

A leader in an urban district was struggling to improve test scores. Based on her evaluation of the districts' results and their gaps, reading needed major focus.

Step 2: Analyze causality

She spoke with many teachers in the district to get their opinion and feedback. She heard from the high school teachers that they thought they did not need to teach reading because they were focused on subject areas and the students should already know

(Continued)

(Continued)

how to read. The leader had recently been working on the science of reading implementation and realized that its principles could be applied to any subject area and be effective.

Step 3: Envision the decision's overall structure

She saw the problem not as individual parts but by understanding that the learning of all subjects is critical for students. She also saw reading as a foundation and through line for learning no matter what the subject a teacher was covering. The teachers had a blind spot, believing that they were teaching math or science and not seeing that reading must be improved for learning. She convinced teachers who said, "It's not my problem," that the student needed to improve reading to achieve learning as the outcome.

Step 4: Achieve resolution

She decided to take some of the principles of the science of reading to build into each subject area, which was an integral part of increasing test scores at the high school level. If the teachers were told they were working on the science of reading as an initiative, they would have resisted and felt insulted. However, building the concepts and principles of the science of reading into the work change the perspective and streamlined the work.

If all staff were integrative thinkers, they would have been more open to bringing in the science of reading into the district, and there could have been a more direct and open process for improvement. The leader could have been more transparent about her approach.

The superintendent and their central office team need to help principals learn how to integrate reading into all subjects and work on best practices from teachers who are integrative thinkers and who can help others. The use of one program for improving results is never an answer for an integrative thinker. A program can be part of an approach, but other factors must become part of a strategy for success. This is why the current approach of separating reading may not be achieving the results it should.

The evaluation of LETRS in Mississippi found that teacher knowledge and quality of instruction increased in Mississippi schools after the training. But teachers in Mississippi didn't just get the training. They also had a system of coaching to support them in applying it—figuring out how what they were learning should translate into practice. (Schwartz, 2022)

The teacher's ownership of the work, the consideration of the time it takes to go in depth with students, and the management of other administrative demands are all factors in implementation. The state initiatives on the science of reading tend to leave out the noncontent factors that create sustainable change and improvement. The integrative leader saves their energy and time and resists the temptation to complain to the state about the lack of integration. Instead, they create strategies that take all instructional and organizational issues into account. The integrative leader will focus on the whole, not the parts. The integrative thinker considers the stress of the teachers, the role of the parents, the teachers' schedule, and other factors that take away time for teachers to implement a new strategy. The challenge is to answer the conventional leaders that care only about their silos. Reports can be written to meet the compliance requirements that can be pulled out of a comprehensive system plan. Only report on the minimal aspects they care about to the people who are holding you accountable. Focus your report on the results for students, and address the areas of legislation that are part of your strategy. As I always say, "Get a C in compliance so you can get an A in results." As stated earlier, our research has shown that low compliance and low rule-following leaders consistently get better results. The same applies to the teachers who focus on each student and their learning, not the separate initiatives.

Our pivot in leadership will not be to implement the science of reading in a silo but to build it into all aspects of learning. Literacy is a strategic lever for all students to learn. Additionally, new legislation on dyslexia in one state is not integrated with the science of reading or even special education. It is required to have a separate plan. Integrative leaders would integrate the legislation into reading and special education with no new committee and no separate plan. Your overall plan for students in reading should address dyslexia, and you can extract the dyslexia aspects out of your special education and/or reading plan and send it to the state.

[illegible] Academics

Integrative thinking must be applied to a range of controversial topics that have become polarized in education. Integrating DEI and SEL into academics has become politicized in our country, and taking sides for and against the choices has hurt the students, families, and communities. Education often gets caught in the middle of politics. Integrative thinking is a way of not taking sides but instead focusing on one side—the learning for students.

SEL and DEI have become controversial in education. These two important topics have become separate initiatives in most districts with their own training, committees, and practices. Integrative thinking will tie the SEL and DEI into the academic focus (see Chapter 3).

DEFINING KEY TERMS

Equity: The National Equity Project (n.d.) states that equity is achieved when "each child receives what they need to develop to their full academic and social potential." Equity is a controversial separate initiative that has not gained the traction it merits. Separate committees on equity, equity coordinators, equity audits, equity plans, and equity training have not been integrated into the DNA of districts and schools. Equity programs are being criticized nationally and have become a political football. The current separate strategy might unfortunately decrease our focus on equity.

SEL: "The process through which all young people and adults acquire and apply the knowledge, skills, and attitudes to develop healthy identities, manage emotions and achieve personal and collective goals, feel and show empathy for others" (Walker, 2024). SEL work has been moving down the same track as equity. The pandemic has put a spotlight on the social-emotional needs of students and staff. Mental health issues are rising in schools at a rapid rate, and staff cannot keep up with their needs. School violence has added an extra element to the fact that students and staff do not feel emotionally and/or physically safe.

CHANGING THE PARADIGM

All these separate programs, although having some success are difficult to maintain and often distract teachers from academic work. Many of these programs emerged when educational funding was strong. The future of funding in education is a concern, and many of these initiatives may lose funding, which can curtail their impact. The political environment is polarizing these initiatives and making it next to impossible to stay focused on the children. DEI programs are losing ground in some states and are being eliminated.

If we integrate and do not separate (see Figure 2.2), we will change the paradigm and the path forward for SEL and equity. The focus would be academic excellence for students or student success, and both equity and SEL would provide information and context on who the students are and what is needed to support them to be successful.

2.2 The Intersection at the Heart of Student Success

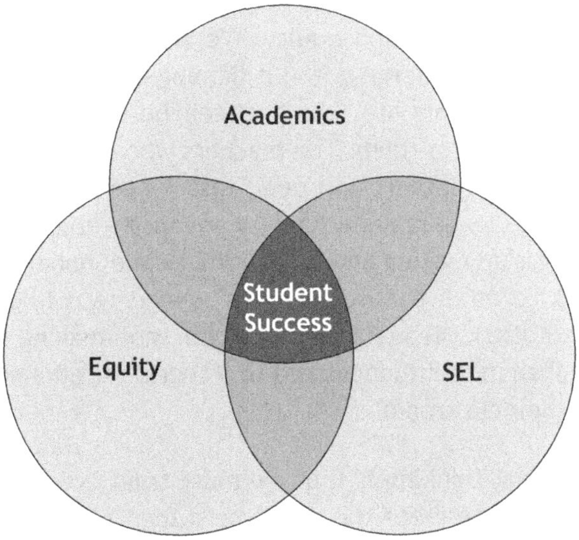

The goal of academics would be the North Star, and equity and SEL will be part of the work every day in every situation to understand the people and how their lives and backgrounds affect their work. Equity and SEL coordinators who have the best intent are often frustrated that they cannot do this work alone. Although the training is well intended, the districts that provide it still see regular problems with SEL and equity issues that are not being addressed.

PIVOT YOUR LEADERSHIP USING INTEGRATIVE THINKING

Begin by focusing on student success, which will be defined as the North Star in Chapter 3. Once student success is clear, you do not need to have equity and SEL committees. In addition, you do not need separate SEL and equity plans. If you focus on student achievement with high expectations for all students, which will be further explained in Chapter 6, you will see how equity and SEL will emerge in every situation every day. For example, try discussing how a fourth-grade class of students are achieving in any district. Once we determine that a student is not achieving, the conversation needs to move to why. If we look at the problem beyond conventional thinking, we will naturally move away from content to who the student is. Are there problems in their life and within their family? What is the student's background, race, ethnicity, and identity? If we know the students, SEL and Equity will expand the story to understand the problem.

Our strategy of helping the student succeed must address all three areas: academics, SEL, and equity. We start with academics, and equity and SEL will emerge without naming them because we must know who the students are. The best teachers know their students and connect to each of them. The teachers who engage students have fewer discipline problems and need less focus on classroom management. "Wise leaders know that to advance equity, they need to distribute decision making and responsibility and mobilize staff members to work together toward solutions" (Noguera & Noguera, 2023). If school and district leaders distribute decision-making to teachers, teachers will then feel empowered to integrate academics, SEL, and equity into their classroom.

Our conventional thinking is that we must train everyone on equity and SEL so they can meet the needs of students. The reality is that genuine conversations do not happen in real life and the training is too theoretical. The assumption is that once trained, the educators will apply the learning. A good leader using integrative thinking realizes that people are too stressed to integrate these concepts. The training is too removed from real-life situations, and the belief systems of staff may not align to ensure consistent implementation.

An integrative leader would use empathy to connect equity and SEL to academic success. If we are empathetic, we seek to understand people's backgrounds and personal challenges. We do not judge them when we empathize; we build relationships and a more in-depth knowledge of root causes that are affecting the student's learning. Through nonjudgmental conversations we can bring in the support that a student needs to succeed. This applies to staff too. If we make judgments about why a staff member is not doing what we want them to do, we may miss the root cause of the problem. Instead of judging them and writing them up for poor performance, we work to understand what is getting in their way. We do not need to sympathize with them or say we have similar challenges. We instead stay the course of a results focus and high expectations with a side-by-side continuous learning relationship to help the person succeed.

The understanding of root causes and not judging adults also applies to students. Be careful not to assume why a students is not connecting to the work in the manner that you think they should. Determine what motivates them to learn first.

Students in general want to integrate and apply their learning to real life. Students of color are even more inclined to be result oriented and potentially be integrative in their thinking (Chapter 5). Unfortunately, our siloed conventional system affects these student's ability to be successful. Conventional thinking is that the teacher is the expert imparting knowledge onto the students. The students become disconnected because they are trying to apply the learning to their experience.

As one principal has stated, it seems the only time we help students apply their learning to real life is when there are problems in their behavior. She continued:

> We make education relevant for students and their life experience only when a student is "in trouble" and we need to discipline the student. We tend to believe that relevance is important to the students who are struggling. Perhaps we should apply relevance to all students in our tier one education efforts.

SAVING MONEY, LESS POLITICAL BACKLASH, AND INCREASING STUDENT AND STAFF LEARNING

As stated earlier, DEI and SEL need to be integrated with academics and leadership. A superintendent started his new role as executive director of a special education collaborative organization in the Northeast. The collaborative previously had used a consultant to provide DEI training over two years at a cost of $200,000. Although there was some benefit in the increased diversity of staff through recruitment, there was dissatisfaction with the limited practical results of the initiative. In addition, some staff felt attacked and that their viewpoints were not valued.

(Continued)

(Continued)

The superintendent embraced the integration concept and stopped doing the DEI work as a separate initiative. Instead, he brought in DEI and SEL as integral parts of the leadership development work for his leadership team and extended managers.

As the leadership team clarified their North Star around student success, challenges and barriers were discussed to develop a plan to move forward. As the team discussed their goals, concerns about how to hire and develop a strong workforce emerged as the number one challenge.

The team noted that staff were focused on tasks, not results. The team used leadership assessments (Indigo [DiSC & Values]) to understand their strengths, areas for improvement, and values. As they discussed staff concerns and problems, they did not need to bring up SEL or DEI separately in the discussion. The DEI and SEL factors emerged naturally in the discussion without being introduced separately. One manager noted that one conflict was being on time all the time versus being on time wherever possible. How can leadership hold onto what appeared as contradictory concepts in their heads without choosing one solution? The answer was to talk to the staff members about the North Star and outcomes for students. Two staff members explained that in their culture being on time was not critical. Together it was discussed why it was important to be on time for students and that work needs to be completed for the budget and board meetings. Once it was clear what the expectations were for being on time and staying focused on deadlines, the SEL and DEI issues could be addressed by adding additional support where needed without changing the expectations.

Now with an integrated approach, SEL and equity are part of solving organizational problems. The team can focus on the results for students and still support the needs of staff. It is not either/or; they can do both.

One major question on this integrative approach is, what do you do if all the leaders are the same as far as race, gender, ethnicity, and identity? How do they bring in different viewpoints if the staff or leadership is not diverse? If a leader is working on their leadership and trying to improve the social orientation score on the WPI, they would establish a network of diverse leaders who help them expand their viewpoints. Networking and learning from others will help them broaden their perspective.

Once we realize that we must embrace and value diversity, we need to recruit, retain, and develop a diverse staff that will be explored in the talent management chapter. We must remember that we are preparing our students to live and work not only in their current community but within a global world. Our new virtual world has accelerated the concept that we can live anywhere but work everywhere. The boundaries and limitations are different today.

In addition, a focus on empathy allows us to listen and understand. Educators need to learn to be empathetic with students and staff to build relationships and discuss the elephants in the room that block genuine strategies for success. Unfortunately, when some people hear empathy, they think the concept is too much about relationships and not about results in areas such as math and science. A strong integrative thinker sees empathy as a means to an end, not the result. If we are empathetic to staff, we connect to their concerns about not having enough time to do their work.

The best way to find time in education is to improve your integrative thinking and the implementation process. Integrative thinking will gain focus and decrease initiatives and distractions.

POSITIVE RESULTS

Here is what you can expect from better integrative thinking and its relationship to implementation:

1. You can respond to emails or phone calls within 24 hours.
2. There can be less of a need to cancel meetings or miss appointments.
3. Meetings will be clearer and shorter with a focus on the North Star.
4. Communication will improve with more focus and fewer initiatives and meetings.
5. Systems follow-through will improve, which will decrease time needed on compliance.
6. Deadlines will be met more frequently. Fewer reminders will be necessary.
7. You can set up backup people to follow through if someone is out.

8. It will be clear who is leading aspects of the work toward the desired results.
9. You can be more proactive and planful with fewer last-second requests.

If you have a smaller number of goals to implement, you will need fewer committees, fewer people involved, less paperwork to track actions, and more time to work on strategic issues and be more proactive. Integrative thinking will save you time, get better results for students, navigate the political waters more effectively, and decrease your stress. Commit to this work, and you are ready for the next chapters to put this approach in motion. To practice, try filling out this integrative thinking worksheet applying integrative thinking to real issues in your district and school.

INTEGRATIVE THINKING WORKSHEET

1. Choose a problem where there are two or more viewpoints on how to solve it.

   Describe the problem:

   Viewpoint 1:

   Viewpoint 2:

2. Identify the outcome you want for students when the problem is solved.

   Outcome for students:

3. What would be the positive outcomes of each viewpoint?

   Positive outcome of viewpoint 1:

   Positive outcome of viewpoint 2:

4. What would be the concerns or negative outcomes for each viewpoint?

   Potential negative outcome of viewpoint 1:

   Potential negative outcome of viewpoint 2:

5. How could you incorporate the positive side of each viewpoint into your plan to get to the desired outcome?

   Ways to incorporate viewpoint 1:

   Ways to incorporate viewpoint 2:

6. How would you address the concerns or negatives of each viewpoint into your plan?

   Ways to address concerns regarding viewpoint 1:

   Ways to address concerns regarding viewpoint 2:

CHAPTER SUMMARY

Learning and committing to integrative thinking are key skills for pivoting leadership to meet the challenges in education. There are too many separate initiatives, that is, silos within districts that take up too much time and do not provide a direct path to improving student outcomes. The skill to look at your North Star and determine how the separate initiatives are tied to student achievement are critical factors for success. Mitigating the overwhelmed and reactive environment in education that causes stress for all staff is necessary and is a result of integrative thinking.

I've provided training for teacher leadership on integrative thinking as a basic skill for focusing on student achievement and saving time on disconnected initiatives. The educational system will continue to provide separate topics and agendas to districts and schools. Education administration at a federal and state levels is too siloed to integrate the work before it is sent to districts. Each separate initiative, for example DEI or SEL, cannot succeed on its own. Concepts and skills taught in a vacuum will have minimal effect on results and often are not sustainable.

Therefore, district or school educators need to integrate before they implement. This process, as outlined in this chapter, will be successful if a district commits to applying integrative thinking as an aspect of all their work. The pivots outlined in the following chapter will be most effective if integrative thinking is a basic skill within the workforce.

CHAPTER TAKEAWAYS

- Embrace Complexity: Accept that complex problems may require complex solutions. Find the common goals and outcomes for the separate initiatives in your district. Streamline your committees and meetings to work on the goals and outcomes, not the separate initiatives. Develop one plan for the goal that incorporates the initiatives' purposes into one plan.
- Be Open-Minded: Stay open to new ideas, and be willing to challenge your assumptions. Accept different points of view as valid. Develop outcomes and plans that build in different viewpoints toward common goals
- Collaborate: Work with others to leverage their knowledge and perspectives. Understand that other viewpoints you may not value or agree with are important. Implementation and commitment

will be bett
viewpoint.

- Stay Patient
processes tc
deal with ea
strategies w
others. It m
to the goal.

QUESTIONS FOR REFLECTION

1. How is integrative thinking more difficult than how you would normally work toward solving a problem?
2. What fears do you have if you focused your work with leaders on developing integrative thinking skills?
3. Do you agree that integrative thinking can help you improve results and save time? If so, find an example to see if it helps you achieve a more effective result.
4. How would you explain this approach to other leaders in your district or school?

3

FINDING YOUR NORTH STAR

Learning Intentions

1. Understand why we need a North Star to guide school districts to improve focus and decrease stress and turnover.
2. Learn a new, streamlined strategic planning process, what it looks like, and how it is aligned with student success.
3. Develop and use your North Star for each district and school to use time more effectively, decrease stress, and improve student success.

What Is the Problem We Are Trying to Solve?

It is essential that teachers and school leaders have a clear definition of what success for students looks like so that they can focus instructional strategies to achieve maximum results for students. The problem is that there are a myriad of directives, initiatives, and mandates that have been prescribed to schools on how to educate our students. Although well intentioned, they have been presented in silos and have created a confusing message for the people closest to the students. These teachers, principals, and district administrators need clarity and focus to provide the best education our children deserve.

The COVID-19 pandemic increased the demands and stress on the educational system, which has created more fragmentation and confusion. These demands have increased stress for teachers, administrators, and parent, who need to work as a team to prepare students for postsecondary education and life. Chapter 1 validated that teacher stress levels are high and have an impact on their retention and ability to help students be successful.

It is time to find a way to focus and simplify the world for educators. As Michael Fullan said, "the concept of 'simplexity' refers to the smallest number of potentially interrelated elements that feed on each other and achieve success" (Fullan & Quinn, 2015). To achieve simplexity, the world of education, which is complex, must be simplified for students to become prepared for life's challenges.

A core component of the confusion and struggle for educators stems from whether standardized tests, which measure academic learning, should be their focus. Some feel that these tests are too narrow and do not measure the skills and competencies that students need to live and thrive in today's world, let alone tomorrow's. A movement has emerged for soft skills, or 21st century skills, saying that education needs a broader focus than only academic standardized test scores. However, test score advocates have continually stated that soft skills are not easily measured using a numerical value.

Unfortunately, instead of integrating standardized tests and essential soft skills, we have continued to add initiatives and strategies to try and gain focus. These resulting separate and unintegrated strategies have increased the problem because we are not clear on our intended results. It is difficult to get into a car to drive somewhere if we do not know where we are going or why we want to get there.

What Is Our Proposed Solution?

We need to develop a clear definition of success for students. There are a few approaches to define student success beyond state standardized tests. Michael Fullan is working with the University of Melbourne, Australia, on New Metrics for Success, a project defining the six Cs (competencies) for success. Roman Sterns (2024), executive director of Scaling Students Success, has also noted in a recent white paper titled *A Student-Centered Approach to Education* that it is time to develop new metrics for student success. Sterns has stated that although graduation rates have increased, standardized tests remain relatively flat, and chronic absenteeism is near an all-time high. He has further stated that too many students do not find school to be interesting, engaging, or relevant to their future. This is particularly true for kids of color and other marginalized populations. Sterns (2024) has recommended the Portrait of the Graduate process to drive the change in the definition of student success., noting that fifteen states are moving in that direction.

We support using the Portrait of the Graduate as an approach for developing one North Star based on an existing process for high school accreditation. The New England Association for Schools and Colleges (NEASC), along with the other accreditation associations across the country, has added the Portrait of a Graduate (also called a Vision of the Graduate) to their standards for accreditation. The accreditation process is used by most high schools, which in turn carry a banner that they are accredited by a reputable third party. The Portrait of a Graduate represents a school or district's vision for the academic skills, 21st century skills, character traits, and social-emotional competencies that students need to succeed in college, career, and life. Vocational schools should use the Portrait of a Graduate process to integrate technical and academic arenas and integrate what they would call employability skills into the framework for academic and technical success.

The challenge that the Portrait of the Graduate solves is the struggle to integrate academic learning and essential skills. In addition, we must bring together all the constituencies to agree with the focus so we can align our educational goals and resources to reach our desired outcomes. The Portrait of the Graduate can do this, becoming the basis for a new strategic planning process that will get results. Strategic planning has been a major approach to gain clarity and focus on education for years. Developing a vision, mission, goals, and strategies with action plans for implementation is our traditional process for decreasing fragmentation and clarifying direction. However, without a North Star it has not been fully successful.

In education, a North Star represents a guiding vision that directs the priorities, decisions, and actions of an educational system or institution. Much like the North Star has historically served as a reliable navigation point, the educational North Star helps educators, administrators, and policymakers stay focused on their ultimate purpose—typically the success and well-being of all students. This vision often encompasses principles such as equity, lifelong learning, critical thinking, and readiness for college, career, and civic life.

Establishing a North Star combines the elements of strategic planning with the Portrait of the Graduate. On its own strategic planning can take too long and bog down the process. I have facilitated more than a hundred strategic plans for districts and hundreds of subsequent strategic plans for schools. While conducting analysis of the plan's effect on student achievement (which can take up to a year), I have noticed that the outcomes for student achievement tend to be minimal as measured by standardized tests.

In education, integrating all the initiatives may seem formidable, but it is essential for creating a coherent system that allows the space to focus on your North Star. What follow are some suggestions on how to begin.

STEPS FOR FOCUSING ON YOUR NORTH STAR

Step 1: Review existing initiatives, and understand their objectives, target areas, and intended outcomes.

Step 2: Identify the common goals or themes across all the initiatives.

Step 3: Prioritize goals based on your district's or school's needs and the needs of your students.

Step 4: Create an implementation action plan, and identify strategies and timelines.

Step 5: Build collaborative partnerships across all constituencies (i.e. educators, administrators, policymakers, community members, and students).

Step 6: Align your resources to your implementation plan.

Step 7: Communicate effectively with all your constituencies.

Step 8: Monitor and adjust based on feedback. You must be willing to adjust as needed based on feedback and evidence of implementation.

INITIATIVE INTEGRATION WORKSHEET

Step 1: Reviewing Existing Initiatives

List all relevant educational initiatives, policies, and mandates at the local, state, and national levels.

Initiative1:

Initiative 2:

Initiative 3:

Summarize the outcomes desired for each initiative.

Initiative 1 outcomes:

Initiative 2 outcomes:

Initiative 3 outcomes:

Step 2: Identifying Common Goal

Identify common goals or themes across different initiatives.

Common goal/themes 1:

Common goal/themes 2:

Common goal/themes 3:

Step 3: Prioritizing Goals

Determine which goals are most important for your district or school.

Priority goal 1:

Priority goal 2:

Priority goal 3:

Step 4: Integration Plan

Develop a plan to integrate policies to achieve common goals. List the strategies to integrate. (A note: Depending on your plan, you may need more or less than three strategies, action steps, or timelines. The goal is to integrate the priority goals. One strategy could hit several priority goals and one action could hit more than one strategy.)

Strategy 1:

Strategy 2:

Strategy 3:

(Continued)

(Continued)

List the actions needed to integrate to achieve the common goals.

Action 1:

Action 2:

Action 3:

Add a timeline for implementation for each of the strategies needed to integrate the policies.

Month/year 1:

Month/year 2:

Month/year 3:

Step 5: Collaborative Partnerships

Identify key stakeholders and partners for collaborative work.

Educators:

Administrators:

Policymakers:

Parents:

Community members:

Others:

Step 6: Resources Alignment

Identify and align necessary resources to support integration efforts.

Funding:

Staff:

Training:

Technology:

Others:

Step 7: Monitoring and Adjustment

Establish mechanisms for monitoring process and adjusting.

Data collection:

Feedback mechanisms:

Evaluation criteria:

Others:

Step 8: Communication

Develop a communication plan to keep internal and external stakeholders informed and engaged.

A NEW SUPERINTENDENT USES THE NORTH STAR TO BRING COHERENCE TO HIS SCHOOLS

In 2023 Jason Sample assumed the role of superintendent of Gateway Community Charter Schools (GCC) in Sacramento, California, which has nine schools and more than 5,500 students. Sample began as a member of the board and then became the director of community relations. He then succeeded Dr. Cindy Peterson after her more than twenty years of effective leadership. Sample began his tenure with the same challenge as any new superintendent faces: How can I build on the success of the previous administration and put my own stamp on where we need to go in the next phase of our development?

Sample, who has a nontraditional educator background, needed to determine how his perspective could work in relation to the instructional focus of an educational system. His first thought was to reach out to all constituents, internal and external, and listen. We introduced him to the Portrait of the Graduate planning process. Sample became excited immediately because of the focus his customers or constituents, which was more in line with his background in district communications and community relations.

Once Sample understood the Portrait of the Graduate, he adopted the concept of coherence. Coherence as defined by Michael Fullan "consists of the shared depth of understanding about the purpose and nature of the work. Coherence, then, is what is in the minds and actions of people individually and especially collectively" (Fullan & Quinn, 2015). Now Fullan could define success based on the skills and competencies that students needed when graduating from GCC. He could back-plan all the internal systems and structure them to align to the needs of the students. He was also excited that the process could be comprehensive, moving much faster than traditional strategic planning, and that GCC schools could be united under a common North Star. The other benefit was that he could get alignment and coherence while still providing independence to school leaders and allowing them to be innovative and focus on the uniqueness of their schools in how to reach the overall North Star for the students and families they serve.

(Continued)

(Continued)

Jason Sample started the Portrait of a Graduate by asking each constituent group, "What are the skills and competencies that students need for postgraduation, learning, and life?" He polled the school board, municipal government leadership, chamber of commerce, key nonprofit leaders, parent organizations, and other key leaders and groups in the community. The answers he received began the process to distill the skills for students down to five to seven essential competencies. These competencies were then integrated into the academics for the district, as measured by the standardized state test (SBACK in California), and formed the North Star.

This process was completed in less than a month. The ownership and buy-in of the Portrait of a Graduate was achieved by gaining input from administrators and teachers as they moved toward implementation. Genuine ownership does not always have to occur before implementation. These two seemingly contradictory statements can be realized by understanding that people can gain a connection to an idea or concept as they implement. The notion that you can move ahead quickly on implementation and gain ownership at the same time is an example of integrative thinking. Because the Portrait of a Graduate is revised through input from teachers and other key groups, implementation can begin right away. Integrating input and feedback from implementors means looking at the original ideas and the feedback. After reviewing feedback from implementors you can look at how these ideas overlap and have common themes that should always tie to the North Star.

The example Portrait of a Graduate (Figure 3.1) has six areas that may be too broad and hard to implement separately. However, through integrative thinking, academic achievement can become the North Star. The academically ready component can include state standardized tests as well as essential skills.

3.1 Gateway Community Charters' Portrait of the Graduate

Portrait of the Graduate					
Academically Ready	Workforce & College Ready	Global Citizens	Life Ready	Productive Citizens	Reflective Citizens
Lifelong leader	Skills & competencies	Culturally & socially respectful	Adaptable	Problem-solver	Curious
Content knowledge	Professional communicators	Service oriented	Self-aware	Cooperative & collaborative	Growth mindset
Digital literacy	Innovative & creative	Responsible	Financially aware	Leader & advocate	Plans for the future
Critical thinker			Empathetic		

Moving to Implementation of the North Star as the Basis for Goal Setting

The six separate initiatives can be collapsed into one; we do not need six plans for implementation. We don't need six new committees; we need only the current structures to begin implementation.

Many districts and schools have instructional leadership teams as umbrella leadership teams. Instruction is the key to success, but forming a leadership team as an umbrella team with instruction and implementation as subset areas of focus will be more effective to reach your North Star (see Figure 3.2). It is important to understand that instruction is the means to student achievement, not the result. Making sure that instruction leads to results requires leadership and implementation. If a school leader focuses on overall leadership, making sure that the follow-through and implementation are effective, their student achievement will increase.

3.2 Leadership Aligned With Instructional Leadership and Management

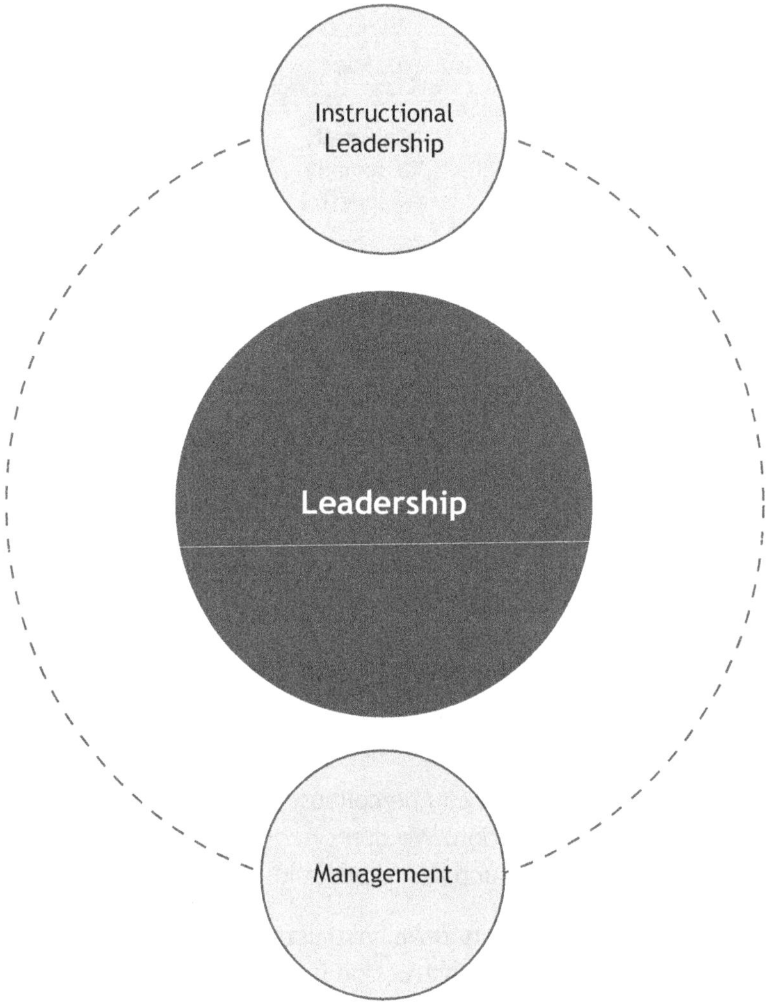

"Although the core service in education is instruction for students, the leader's role is to ensure that the highest quality of service is provided. The instructional services must be provided in an effective and efficient manner and need to be sustainable and adaptable over time" (Kirtman, 2014).

One principal recently stated that he liked the focus on leadership and that the instructional leadership and the management (implementation) components were subsets; however, it seemed counterintuitive. It is counterintuitive because we have been taught that the only focus should be on instruction in the classroom. However, if we do not broaden our focus, crisis and reactionary issues take us away from instructional focus. The principal agreed that if the school was managed properly, and he was leading and working with administrators in his school and at the district level effectively, there would be more time to concentrate on instruction. Principals should own everything but not do everything. This requires a partnership with the central office and the support of schools leader to get results. Being less top-down and more service oriented will result in sustainable improvement. Maybe this is counterintuitive too, but it works.

STEPS FOR FORMING ONE COMMITTEE

Step 1: Form your leadership team of administrators and teachers. You can also add other classified and unclassified staff to your team. One school added their administrative assistant, whereas another added their head custodian. Keep the team a manageable size of eight to ten people if possible.

Step 2: Define the role of the leadership team as working alongside the principal to help lead all aspects of the school. The principal will have the ultimate authority, but distributing leadership to other members of the team is powerful for improved results. The concept of distributive leadership is more powerful than delegation alone because it creates ownership, not task orientation.

Step 3: List all the district and the school initiatives (use the worksheet earlier in the chapter).

Step 4: Determine how these initiatives connect to the North Star.

Step 5: If an initiative does not connect to the North Star, take the elements that connect, and decrease your focus on the aspects that are not aligned.

(Continued)

(Continued)

Step 6: Set up monthly team meetings limited to 90–120 minutes so the whole team can discuss key challenges or problems.

Step 7: The first hour of the meetings can cover general goals and strategies that affect the whole school them move toward success as defined in the North Star.

Step 8: The remainder of the time, the team can decide on subgroup work. For example, a subgroup could examine data to recommend strategies to improve reading. This subgroup would have a small number of outside meetings to bring back recommendations to the whole leadership team.

Step 9: The team will record action items and always look at measurements as they review subgroup work.

Step 10: The leadership team can rotate membership to provide more opportunities for staff to be part of leadership over time.

An example of this involves the science of reading. The states often prescribe forming a separate committee, plan, and a prescribed program directed by the Department of Education. States often recommending excellent content but move too far into how to implement, resulting in a silo.

If the science of reading is a core aspect of the leadership team's work, implementation will be more effective. Reading is fundamental to learning in other subject areas, so the plan for success, which will be both academic and essential skill driven, can involve science and math teachers using the fundamental aspects of reading to improve math and science scores. Essential skills such as critical thinking can be linked as well to help students improve life skills and test scores.

This approach decreases the number of meetings needed. It also decreases the time principal s need to lead and attend these meetings. The leadership team can become more strategic and integrative, helping the principal have more time to connect with and coach teachers.

As the GCC's superintendent began to implement the Portrait of the Graduate, he received input that although he was attempting to integrate, not separate, the Portrait of the Graduate, it still seemed to have silos. Based on staff and consultants input, he revised the Portrait of the Graduate to explain the North Star (see Figure 3.3).

3.3 Integration of the Portrait of the Graduate

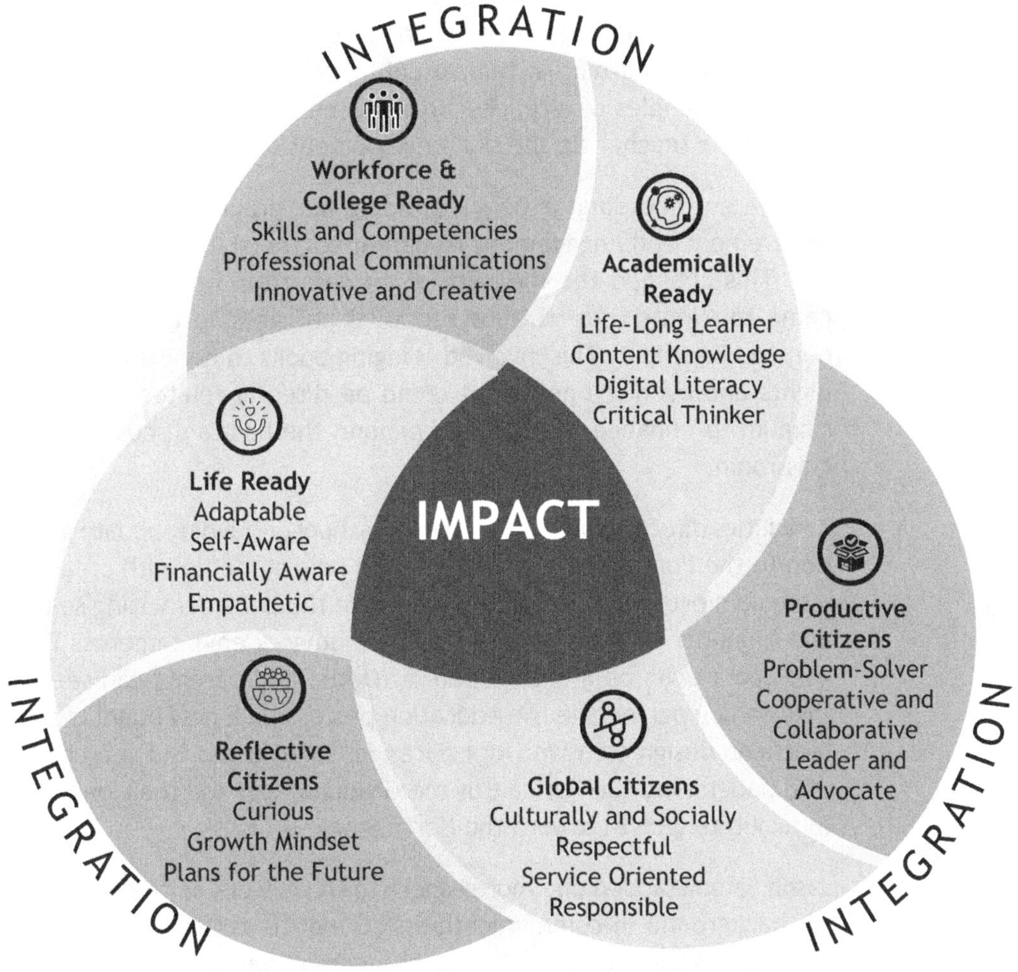

Source: Jason Sample

Each school and district department then developed goals on how they could play an integral part in moving GCC toward the North Star. For example, under Life Ready is a bullet that states that students need to be financially aware. One math teacher built financial management into her math classes. This is a great example of integrating academics with an essential skill. It doesn't require an additional class or program; it is built into an existing class by developing a lesson plan that integrates both.

A Career and Technical Education (CTE) Programs leader who was building a separate college and career ready program instead collaborated with the instructional coaches on tying the essential skills in the North Star to increase academic learning. This involved adding in the essential skills to the instructional rounds that the instructional coaches make on a regular basis. The instructional coach could review the academic learning in their usual manner. In addition, they could look for examples of a teacher focusing on critical-thinking skills and helping the teacher tie the skill development of learning math.

The parent coordinator began building her program beyond parent involvement and engagement to parent partnership in student learning. This changed the measure of success from how many parents came to events to a true instructional partnership to improve student achievement. This involved bringing books to review for parents' nights and events, books that could be directly related to the curriculum to enhance the learning beyond the basics discussed in the classroom.

A facilities director can look at any new school or building update in relation to the Portrait of the Graduate. To help students with creativity, more comfortable spaces can be set up in the classroom using seating, and small corners can be used as informal work environments. These workspaces can be great for parent nights, and parents can see how they can be partners in the education process. In a new building architects can design creative workspaces for small group work—architects who understand the Portrait of the Graduate can add their own ideas to facilitate growth toward the North Star.

Jason Sample added one more aspect to GCC's work on the North Star. His background in communications led him to ask each principal to develop a video for parents and the community on how they were integrating essential skills and academics in each of their schools. Each video would involve students, teachers, and staff. His plan of showing his vision through a video provided direction and accountability for all staff to stay on course toward the Portrait of the Graduate.

Putting the North Star to Work

The North Star must be the focus of every meeting. Each meeting or discussion needs to determine how the work ahead advances the school or district to the North Star. If the subject doesn't advance toward the outcome, it needs to get less or no attention. If it is compliance oriented and not connected to the North Star, as I always say, "Get a C in compliance." "Compliance requirements often derail the work of consistent improvement in schools" (Fullan & Kirtman, 2019).

Delegate the work, and complete it quickly. Peter DeWitt (2022a) has talked about the process of de-implementation, which reduces work that has little effect on student learning. This allows teachers to concentrate on deeper and more impactful practices. He outlined four areas for reducing low-impact work: partial reduction, complete reversal, substitution with related replacement, and substitution with unrelated replacement of existing practice. Although this process sounds complicated, his book, *De-Implementation: Creating the Space to Focus on What Works,* will guide you through the process (Dewitt, 2022a).

Another example of reducing compliance work is from a student services leader who separates compliance tasks from leadership or management tasks. The compliance task can be checking the box on an assurance requirement from the state. The leadership task is to analyze student data to determine the high-leverage areas for student achievement. The management task is to ensure that the right people are analyzing the data and reporting to leaders with suggestions for actions or questions that need more exploration.

Every issue needs to have the North Star as a lens. For example, special education has an inordinate amount of compliance requirements and is focused on process more than student outcomes. The Individualized Education Plan (IEP) is a staple for the work in special education. In essence the IEP has become a North Star. However, the IEP is not the outcome but rather a process that provides needed services to students who are designated for special education services.

When most districts look at results on standardized tests, they see major gaps in achievement for special education students. If the North Star were used for special education, it would change the expectations for staff and students. For example, a special education teacher would look at student success for all students first before completing the IEP. The North Star defines student success for academic achievement and for life. The IEP would be the plan to get to the North Star.

Communicating Internally and Externally to Connect to Everyone

With all our great technological advances, the age-old problem of communication is still a major concern in most districts. It is interesting that communication problems exist in suburban, rural, and urban issues. Communication is even more of a problem with parents, municipal leaders, and the community. We recommend that marketing, communication, and public relations be part of everyone's job, not only the superintendent. Most administrative preparation programs spend little time on marketing and communication. If they do, they recommend hiring a person to lead communications. Telling your story and establishing the value of your school and district are critical in reaching your North Star. Using the Portrait of a Graduate is a great way to begin the dialogue to discover what is missing between the district and its community.

This lack of communication creates confusion internally in districts, leading to the day-to-day problems outlined in Chapter 2. Lack of communication can cause an even greater problem externally that can even affect district budget allocations. If leaders in the community do not understand the return on investment or how resources affect student success, they could believe any additional resources requested by the superintendent or school board are being wasted. Having the entire community as part of the Portrait of the Graduate process will eliminate this confusion and focus the community's attention on the North Star and the results for students.

STEPS FOR EFFECTIVELY COMMUNICATING YOUR NORTH STAR

Step 1: Build in North Star updates in your newsletters that feature success stories school and district wide.

Step 2: Superintendents should provide regular updates to the school board on the North Star.

Step 3: Build excitement in your schools by featuring students and faculty discussing what the school and the North Star means to them. For example, develop videos where students talk about how they feel about the Portrait of the Graduate.

Step 4: In each evaluation of staff, tie a goal to the Portrait of the Graduate.

Step 5: Feature progress on the Portrait of the Graduate and success stories during each parent night.

Step 6: Talk about the North Star and Portrait of the Graduate with municipal government, community groups, and businesses and during all external meetings and events.

ANAHEIM TAKES THE NORTH STAR TO THE CLASSROOM

The Anaheim Union High School District has fully integrated their North Star into classrooms on a regular basis. Their North Star is defined as a whole child vision. They have three elements that are integrated into one clear direction: their five Cs (essential competencies for students), student voice, and technical skills. The process of developing the North Star has progressed over a six-year period and is still evolving. This North Star's whole child vision is truly a community-driven effort. They held visioning sessions in each school with all staff as participants. They also invited parents and community members into their visioning sessions.

Each visioning session had two questions:

1. What do you think is the purpose of K–12 schools?
2. What skills and competencies do you believe students need for postsecondary education and for life?

All the SESSIONS' answers were pulled together to develop the five Cs and to integrate student voice and technical skills into their framework. All participants engaged in dialogue and reading connected to research on workforce demands. Through this process, the district identified the collective voice of their community, a North Star grounded in whole child education that prepares students to be successful in college, career, and life. Their integrated whole child career preparedness process has had a direct positive effect over time on standards-based state tests (SBAC) because it is aligned to those standards.

The district is working with a higher education partners and the Chan Zuckerberg Institute to utilize artificial intelligence (AI) connected to student reflections to gauge student growth and progress regarding essential skills. The five Cs include character and compassion, collaboration, communication, creativity, and critical thinking. Each student is placed on a rubric for each skill. They have used AI to develop easy access to this information and to improve their ability to assess and improve student achievement in the five Cs. Their success is becoming a model that is gaining national attention.

(Continued)

(Continued)

The student voice element is a core part of this process; students develop capstone projects that integrate the five Cs and technical skills. The technical skills include traditional content standards in addition to the skills connected to many career technical education pathways the district offers, dual credit, and Google certificate integration in specific classes.

Each school develops performance task assessments (PTAs) designed to improve all three aspects of the Career Preparedness system Framework (CPSF), not only the five Cs. However, when students reflect on their work on PTAs, they focus the impact on their growth in the five Cs.

At key times each student is asked to do reflections on how they are progressing on all the aspects of the North Star. Progress toward the standards, the five Cs, and the technical skills, in addition to the student reflections, are entered into the AI platform to refine the PTAs and improve achievement and subsequently results on standards-based tests.

Communication is one of the five Cs for Anaheim (see Figure 3.4). Communication has been defined by the Anaheim Union High School District as "the sharing of ideas, information, opinions, or emotions with other people. Communication can be written, spoken, or nonverbal and requires the ability to read and understand text, write, and speak with clear purpose, tone, and awareness of audience; and listen effectively to others." All aspects have been integrated into Anaheim's school district through its Career Preparedness System Framework, maximizing its internal alignment and infrastructure around three essential drivers: 21st century skills (soft skills), technical skills (hard skills), and cultivation of student voice and purpose (civic skills).

Their focus on the North Star has gained amazing support from the school board, the entire community, and local universities. National foundations have been interested in this process and provided additional funding to support the work of the district. The district believes that focusing on preparing students for career and financial success will allow all constituents to work in a unified, nonpartisan approach, and there have been fewer problems with political issues because of this unifying process.

3.4 Communication Competency Rubric

ANAHEIM UNION HIGH SCHOOL DISTRICT

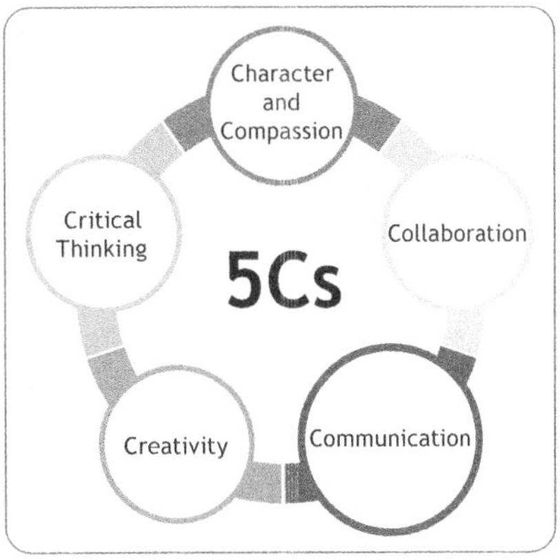

COMMUNICATION

Communication is the sharing of ideas, information, opinions, or emotions with other people. Communication can be written, spoken, or nonverbal and requires the ability to read and understand text; write and speak with clear purpose, tone, and awareness of audience; and listen effectively to others. As technology changes, communication must constantly adapt in school, work, and everyday life, but remains central to the sharing of knowledge and forming of relationships.

	Students who need substantial scaffolding and guidance are: **EMERGING**	Students who need moderate facilitation are: **PROGRESSING**	Students who need minimal direction are: **EXCELLING**
COMPREHENSION	Demonstrate some understanding of information (subject, purpose, audience, relevance, tone).	Demonstrate understanding of information (subject, purpose, audience, relevance, tone) and identify important ideas.	Demonstrate strong understanding of information (subject, purpose, audience, relevance, and tone) from various sources; identify important ideas and supporting details; make connections between information, past learning, or life experiences.
MESSAGE	May need support to clearly convey message and to adjust approach for different writing or speaking situations.	Convey message clearly; attempt to adapt genre and language to the purpose, audience, and medium when writing or speaking.	Convey message articulately and purposefully; independently adapt genre and language to various purposes, audiences, and mediums when writing or speaking.
SPEAKING	May need reminders and support to demonstrate poise, voice, emotion, eye contact, gestures, and appropriate speed when speaking.	Demonstrate poise, voice, emotion, eye contact, gestures, and appropriate speed when speaking.	Effectively engage the audience; consistently demonstrate poise, voice, emotion, eye contact, gestures, and appropriate speed when speaking.
LISTENING	Listen with some understanding; may need scaffolding for positive listening behaviors such as sitting up, leaning forward, asking questions, nodding, and tracking the speaker.	Recognize and restate main points when listening; demonstrate some positive listening behaviors such as sitting up, leaning forward, asking questions, nodding, and tracking the speaker.	Recognize main ideas, make relevant connections, and detect bias when listening; independently employ positive listening behaviors including sitting up, leaning forward, asking questions, nodding, and tracking the speaker.
REFLECTION	Reflect on content of written or oral communication with scaffolding and guidance.	Reflect on content and delivery of written or oral communication.	Reflect on content, delivery, and implications of written or oral communication; identify how learning altered existing knowledge or approach.

CLASSROOMS THAT PROMOTE COMMUNCATION

- Give assignments that allow students to practice different modes of communication (written, oral and nonverbal) and ensure approximately 30% of class time is dedicated to providing formal and informal speaking opportunities.
- Provide opportunities for students to communicate with various audience (peers, teachers, outside audiences) to contextualize communications.
- Use technology to develop speaking and listening skills (e.g., create video blogs that allow students to practice speaking then have students develop their aural skills by listening to each other's video blogs, noting the purpose, main points, implications, and tone).
- Ask open-ended questions to facilitate discussion and debate and demonstrate multiple ways to interpret and answer a question.
- Encourage students to develop their independent voice through freedom of choice in mode and topic.

AUHSD 5CS DESCRIPTOR- COMMUNICATION

Source: Anaheim Union High School District

A third example of how to move ahead with a North Star involves vocational schools. Vocational Schools tend to be focused on the students' technical skills. However, they have been pushed by state mandates and state testing to increase their focus on academics. This tension between the two areas has been difficult because many teachers in vocational schools have traditionally come from the trades. However, because of robotics and medical technologies, many vocational jobs need a combination of academic and technical skills. In addition, essential skills are extremely important in the world of work. These three areas of technical, academic, and essential skills are often in silos. Adding initiatives such as DEI and SEL creates even more siloed non-integrative work for vocational schools. The Portrait of a Graduate provides a way to focus and integrate these separate initiatives into a clear focus for students, staff, and parents. The following is an example of how a vocational school began to develop their North star.

NORTH STAR WORK ENERGIZES A VOCATIONAL SCHOOL

Denise Pigeon, superintendent of Nashoba Valley Technical High School in Westford, Massachusetts, is using the Portrait of a Graduate process to integrate technical and academics with the school's employability skills. Her school has the following employability traits: resilience, respectful, resourceful, responsible, and ready. At first the Portrait of a Graduate process went quickly and gained broad-based support from all staff. It was relatively easy developing employability skills as part of student success (Personal communication, March 2024).

Moving to implementation started out smoothly as staff integrated the employability skills into awards and the overall language used in their school. Unfortunately, it has slowed down and become more complicated as they moved to curriculum and assessment. However, she will be using the new standards from the accreditation process to integrate the more challenging areas such as curriculum development and instruction.

The school will bring teachers in to look at the new standards as they review their curriculums. She will help teachers develop rubrics for integrating the technical and academic aspects of the standards. Pigeon said, "The teachers enjoyed the work because it was relevant to what they believed would make their students successful." The Anaheim rubric and process can work for vocational schools because it is driven by employment. Internal and external stakeholders can review all their documents and use the North Star to show how employers will benefit from hiring students with the essential skills that build on the technical and the academics to create successful workers.

A student who is on time, takes responsibility for their actions, and has strong technical skills and a knowledge of math, science, and English is an ideal worker for any employer. The technically skilled employee who is late to work, cannot work in a team, and does not have basic academic skills will not be successful in the workforce today.

The Portrait of the Graduate process has taken up to a year to get going; however, we believe it can be done more quickly and effectively to serve as a driving force for all systems and practices in a district. As Pigeon stated, "We moved fast at the beginning, but the extra time comes in as we try to simplify all the demands on education, compliance, and assessments that do not measure success based on the Portrait of a Graduate" (Personal communication, March 2024).

Each district can move toward the North Star in their unique manner. The leadership needs to consider the culture of the district, the past work on strategic planning and the needs of their community. Whichever path is taken, the clarity of the North Star will allow your district to align your goals, strategies, and actions to student achievement. As a retired superintendent told me, "The strategic plan or in our new approach the North Star will become a sword and a shield to prevent distractions and maintain the course." All staff, parents, and the community will appreciate simplicity and focus. Initiatives will not become independent programs anymore. Whether an initiative is coming from the staff or from any other party, the content will be integrated into your North Star.

No more separate committees on new initiatives, as we discussed in Chapter 2, should emerge. Less time spent in committee meetings and on initiatives not owned by teachers will allow them to put more of their time into teaching and learning. When teachers hear how a North Star goes beyond test scores into the skills and competencies for students, they breathe a sigh of relief. They feel more grounded and clear about what they are trying to accomplish. This focus relieves teacher stress, which carries over to the students. One teacher recently said to me, "If compliance is my job, you do not need me since there is an art and science to teaching."

The North Star works along with the teacher leadership efforts, which will be discussed in Chapter 4 and will provide a less stressful environment. The effort to focus teachers' time and decrease compliance work that often seems to have no purpose will have a positive effect on teacher retention.

Integrating Social Emotional Learning (SEL) and Equity (DEI) Into Your North Star

Since the pandemic, we have had a substantial increase in mental health issues and behavior problems in education. The response has been SEL curriculums and programs nationally. These programs are important but need to be integrated into the North Star. The North Star of academics informs us on how SEL issues are affecting individual students' learning. If a student is not achieving, there may be SEL issues. We need to help mitigate them in the classroom and with school counselors for support. However, the outcome and measurement for this work is not the SEL curriculum or training; it is student learning. Equity, as stated in Chapter 2, is losing ground nationally based on political divisions and backlash. If the North Star is clear and focused on academics, equity becomes part of the focus for all students and staff. We must stay focused on high expectations and not get distracted by the belief that equity means lowering standards for students or staff. We need to understand how race and identity affect students in the learning process because of their experiences. We then build academics and life skills into the experiences of students of color and into our strategy of excellence. "At the same time, it is important for leaders to make clear that the pursuit of equity is not a rationale for mediocrity, for favoring some groups over others, or for lowering standards and expectations (Noguera & Noguera, 2023).

For example, in an urban district high school, the staff believed that they needed to help students (especially students of color) get out of poverty, not try to meet lofty academic and career goals. They believed this showed they cared for the students. The faculty believed that the goal of SEL meant that the social emotional issues of students were a priority and that high academic expectations would have a negative effect on troubled students; in effect, these expectations would set up false hope. "The schools that make the greatest progress in meeting their equity goals work to create a culture that prioritizes *students'* needs. This means faculty and staff must be curious about students' needs and students' interests" (Noguera & Noguera, 2023). In fact, if the North Star integrated academic and life skills into its Portrait of a Graduate, then the standards would not be lowered for any students. Chapter 5 will further discuss why lowering standards is not acceptable. Equity and SEL affect the path to excellence but not the goal or outcomes.

The North Star combines academic success as measured by statewide standards-based testing and competencies regarding essential skills. Graduates need to have both. School boards and the community must understand how these are integrated. Standardized tests are a minimum requirement for success. If a student chooses to become a landscaper or a plumber, they still need to have math, science, and writing skills. However, academic skills are not enough for life; every student needs to be a creative problem-solver and critical thinker and be resilient to handle life's challenges. The pandemic has proven the importance of being resilient.

The North Star will be effective only if it is measurable. We need measurements to ascertain progress. As we said earlier, Michael Fullan's "simplexity" applies to all aspects of education, including measurements. Currently many districts are using SMARTIE goals (specific, measurable, ambitious, realistic, time-bound, inclusive, and equitable) to evaluate. Overemphasizing "realistic" goals tends to result in goals that are task and not results oriented. We need our goals to be results oriented and aligned to the North Star.

We need to identify one to three measurements as success indicators. A district could have a success indicator of a 10% increase on standardized test scores. Each school then would take a deep look at their student data, determine the largest gap in their scores, and set a percent increase on one area(e.g., 12 percent in math).

One teacher reported that she increased math scores during the school's year of focusing on literacy. She was a true results-oriented and integrative thinker and applied the strategies for literacy for her math classes. She integrated vocabulary development, enhanced reading fluency, and built comprehension skills using word problems. She had the largest increase in math in her district in the year that was not focused on math.

The measurements on your state standardized tests combined with the rubric for the essential skills will provide direction for all staff. In Anaheim they focused on the five Cs and integrated academics into all the classrooms; they have shown subsequent growth on state standardized tests.

I have been working on quantifying essential skills to match and correlate with state tests using artificial intelligence. This could be significant for public policy and create equal value for state standards-based tests and essential skills. Integration is enhanced by both sets of skills becoming quantifiable and equally valuable.

STEPS FOR DEVELOPING AND USING YOUR NORTH STAR

Step 1: Commit to the new strategic planning effort. This commitment should begin with the superintendent and senior cabinet members.

Step 2: Begin interviews and conversations with constituencies including business leaders, community members, teachers, instructional and non-instructional staff, students, and parents. The focus will be on skills and competencies for graduates for postsecondary education and life.

Step 3: Analyze information and feedback from community groups, and draft or update your vision statement, mission statement, and core values. At this point, you create the draft of the Portrait of the Graduate.

Step 4: Development implementation strategies, action plans, success criteria, and monitoring strategies.

Step 5: Each school develops their plan based on the Portrait of a Graduate guided by the vision, mission, and core values.

Step 6: Each central office department will develop their goals and strategies based on the Portrait of the Graduate.

Step 7: All leadership development and professional development will be driven by the Portrait of the Graduate.

Step 8: Gain ownership from your school board and municipal government for the process and results, and describe how the Portrait of the Graduate will affect each political body.

Step 9: Each year the DISTRICT will reevaluate the Portrait of the Graduate to stay current with the trends in the workforce and the overall needs of your students.

Step 10: The Portrait of the Graduate will be your guide to budget priorities. In addition, continue to make it more understandable to parents, municipal leaders, community, and business.

Step 11: The Portrait of the Graduate can be used to develop additional unrestricted revenue for districts. This effort can involve forming a foundation, alumni associations, or avenues for individual and business contributions. It is time for districts to go beyond traditional grant writing for the revenue they need to innovate.

CHAPTER SUMMARY

The North Star will be the focal point for whatever you do in your district or school. There should be no new initiatives that are not integrated into your North Star, and everyone internally and externally will be using the same language to align all resources to improve student achievement. Your North Star needs to integrate the hard skills as measured in state standardized tests and the soft skills that measure the skills students need to be successful in life. Both the hard and soft skills are equally important and critical for success.

Do not let anyone take you off track from your North Star. The North Star focus will enhance your relationship with parents, the community, and all constituencies. All partners should be able to articulate your North Star and how they can play an important role in helping your students be successful. The stress of a myriad of tasks, initiatives, and new programs will be reduced through this focused approach. New ideas and innovations are welcomed if they help your students reach the North Star or if they can be integrated into that North Star.

CHAPTER TAKEAWAYS

- Define results for the district so everyone can state them. Use the Portrait of the Graduate to define the skills and traits of a student needs for success at each level (elementary, middle, and high schools) and how to build these skills throughout their education.

(Continued)

(Continued)

- Set high expectations. Conduct district-wide facilitated grade- and content-level meetings with teachers to discuss the curriculum, review student performance data, and set benchmarks for grade-level assessments.
- Take one of our three examples of a North Star, and use it as a draft for your district. Make it your own, and involve your community.
- Use the rubric from Anaheim to connect the academic and essential skills to the classroom, draft a document, and gain input from teachers.
- Collapse current committees to form leadership teams in your schools and district.
- Present your new North Star to your school board as a more effective approach to gain success for students. This process will help the board focus on results, not day-to-day operations or personal agendas.

QUESTIONS FOR REFLECTION

1. Could staff in our district at all levels explain what our North Star is for our students? What would they say?
2. Could parents, community members, and other constituencies state clearly what our North Star means to them? Try it, and see what they say.
3. How could you as a leader spend more proactive time clarifying your North Star and less time reacting to problems?
4. What are your fears and hesitations on establishing and leading from a clear North Star?

4

MOVING FROM HUMAN RESOURCES TO TALENT MANAGEMENT

Solving the Workforce Crisis

Learning Intentions

1. Understand how to broaden human resources to talent management to address the workforce crisis.
2. Learn how to find, retain, and develop all staff.
3. Build teacher leadership to create sustainable improvement in student achievement.
4. Integrate the components of talent management.

What Is the Problem We Are Trying to Solve?

According to the National Center for Education Statistics (2023b), "Salaries and benefits for staff made up 79 percent of current expenditure costs in

2020-21." Education is a people-oriented business. The function of human resources is about people; however, it has not changed to meet the needs of today's workforce. Education may be facing the greatest challenges it has ever seen. Therefore, it is time to look at how we use budgets to meet these new challenges. Human resources or talent management departments need to be leaders in driving the results for the district. Talent management, as defined by McKinsey & Company, "includes all the ways that organizations bring employees on board, keep them happy and productive, and help them continue to develop their skills over time" (Billing & De Smet, 2023).

The challenge driving the need to change is that conventional approaches to hiring and managing the workforce are not working as well as in the past. The number of qualified people applying for key positions is low. Teachers, school leaders, and district leaders are leaving education at alarming levels. According to McKinsey & Company, 61% of school administrators are having difficulty filling positions (Bryant, 2023). The workforce is so stressed that potential teachers are losing their ability and desire to be educators. According to a 2022 National Education Association survey, 55% of teachers are thinking of leaving the profession (Walker, 2022). The number of people who are attending education schools is also decreasing. The pipeline for the staff we need is drying up. The pressure for compliance and task culture are contributing to superintendents retiring early and the decrease in the number of potential replacement candidates. "The superintendent job has become more difficult in recent years, as political issues infiltrate district leaders' day-to-day work" (Peetz, 2023). In one eastern state, the commissioner (state superintendent) ends the superintendent conference every year with a presentation including a 100-item task list that every superintendent must do. Can you imagine a group of CEOs in the business world being handed a list of tasks to do? The CEOs know their job is about increasing results, and when we start treating superintendents as CEOs, they can focus on their job—*increasing student success.*

The current process for seeking applications, hiring, and dealing with the current workforce requires skills and strategies well beyond the typical background and training of people in human resources departments. Superintendent searches are lucky to have twenty to thirty candidates. According to the National Center for Education Statistics

(2023a), 86% of school districts reported challenges in hiring teaching positions in 2023-2024. Even if there is a reasonable number of candidates, only a small number match the skills and attitudes needed for our new approach.

What Is Our Proposed Solution?

We propose that talent management provide more internally qualified candidates. A talent management strategy helped a superintendent in Arizona recruit a candidate for the director of classified staff. The superintendent knew a strong former teacher who had been a principal but was thinking about a change in role. This leader had family members who worked in classified support roles in maintenance and food service. He approached the candidate to lead the classified staff with a new vision of customer service and connection to student learning. The candidate was qualified on the educational side, and his personal passion for people who worked in classified positions made him an ideal candidate. He never would have applied for the position based on traditional HR practices is now in his new role and bridging the gap between classified and professional staff.

Talent management is a system that helps organizations attract, develop, and retain employees to meet their needs and achieve their goals. It's a strategic approach that involves investing in people as an organization's most important resource. Human resources is the department within an organization that deal with employee matters such as hiring, training, labor relations, and benefits. We highly recommend that your human resource function broadens its focus to talent management. Education must move away from the more passive philosophy to a more proactive recruitment and retaining talent approach. The Wallace Foundation has said,

> Principal effects are broader in scope than those of a teacher because they are felt across an entire school rather than a single classroom. Still, the effects stem in large part from a leader's work with teachers, including how principals hire and coach staff members and create a school environment conducive to learning. (Gill, 2021)

It is becoming difficult to find teachers, principals, special education staff, and almost every role in education. For example, there is a major national bus drivers' shortage. Districts are using traditional methods to advertise for positions. They are even trying to increase salaries because we usually assume money is the ultimate answer. However, the crisis continues. One district in Colorado has practiced real talent management. They are teaming up with an artificial intelligence firm that has determined the best routes with their current bus drivers. They have added trained ride share staff to also help with the problem. They have solved their bus driver crisis and significantly increased the current drivers' salary while saving more than $500,000.

The teacher crisis is the most severe problem facing education. It is important to focus on genuine teacher leadership. Other sectors have realized that the people who are closest to the client or customer need to be able to make decisions. A comprehensive approach to build teacher leadership will help attract and retain great teachers and improve student success. Strategies for partnering with unions and associations for supporting teachers are an integral part of the solution. As one teacher union president told me, "We want more money but realize it will never be enough. However, a teacher's voice is equally important to us!"

The North Star, through the Portrait of the Graduate, will drive the teacher leader program. The Portrait of the Graduate will focus the teachers on what success means for their students. This clear focus will decrease the constant pull from many directions that cause stress. Kate Dias, president of the Connecticut Education Association (the state teacher's union) has agreed that the lack of clarity of results makes a teacher's job stressful and causes confusion and frustration. She further has stated that once teachers are clear about what success is for students and their role in the process of achieving the results, accountability becomes clear. Teachers can and will be leaders both within the classroom and in their school, district, and community. With clarity and a voice, teachers will rise to the occasion.

Talent management is a district-wide effort that should be led by the superintendent. Human resources will also need to realign their systems and structure to a talent management model tied to the Portrait of the Graduate.

New organizational structures are needed to meet the challenges of your Portrait of the Graduate. Talented people will not stay if they are bogged down in menial compliance tasks that distract them from student results as outlined in the Portrait of the Graduate and the North Star.

Chapter 1 defines the skills and behaviors of successful leaders and staff. These data enable a district to identify staff who have the behaviors and skills to assume formal and informal roles as leaders. The data provide helpful information that will guide you in your hiring, development, and retaining of all professional and classified staff. This new perspective on the difficulty in finding and retaining staff in relation to the national workforce crisis shows that if you recruit and develop staff, you will be able to get talented educators.

I have worked with numerous urban, suburban, and rural districts. The challenges and goals are similar to increase student achievement as defined in Chapter 3. The approaches, resource concerns, and politics are all prevalent but different in their application. Urban districts are finding it challenging to find and retain the best talent. The scrutiny of the state and federal government is extreme, and the pressure on the staff is extraordinary. The suburban districts are also struggling to get the best talent. The pressure from parents can make it difficult for educators to work there even though the resources and student issues may appear to be less of a concern. Rural districts have fewer resources and staff but the same goals and outcomes. Rural districts often feel they cannot apply some of the principles of talent management because they have to hire people to do so many different functions. I have found that rural districts can benefit even more from talent management. Because they have less staff, the effects of a poor teacher or administrator are even more of a concern. With no slack in the system, it is almost impossible for others to pick up the responsibilities of an ineffective staff member. Rural districts must have high expectations for every person they hire because the ramifications are even more dramatic than for urban or suburban districts.

Human capital is a term used more in business to note the importance of the people in the organization to the bottom line. In education it should be obvious that people are the key to success for students and families. Unfortunately, education has not been explicit on this point. To that end, Figure 4.1 illustrates the four key steps to effective talent management: 1) Make the case for talent management, 2) develop a plan for recruiting and retaining staff, 3) build sustainable leadership through talent development, and 4) integrate the components of talent management for optimal success.

4.1 The Four Steps to Effective Talent Management

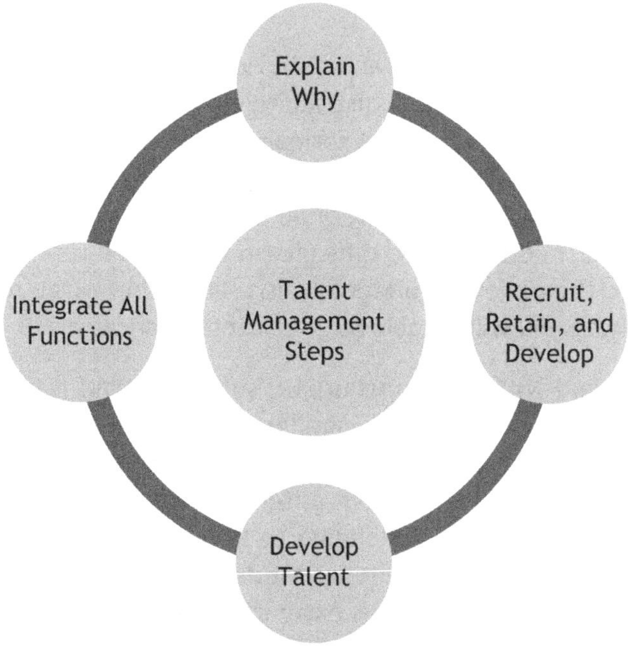

Step 1-Make the Case for Talent Management

When presenting your case to the district or school board for why your school (and district) needs to move to a focus on talent management, the following rationales might be helpful.

MAKING THE CASE FOR A MOVE TO TALENT MANAGEMENT

- ✓ Talent management allows all members of the organization to be responsible for ensuring they are a good fit for the organization. (Fit is a two-way assessment. It must be a fit for the employee and a fit for the organization.)
- ✓ Talent management allows for a direct link to vision, mission, values, and strategy at every point in the employment life cycle.
- ✓ Talent management allows organizations to emphasize environmental fit.

- ✓ Talent management allows staff members to utilize their strengths (what each member is good at) and their values (what each member enjoys) to ensure an effective work-life balance.
- ✓ Talent management requires a collaborative effort among all entities to develop the workforce to meet current and future needs for students.
- ✓ Talent management allows a pathway for staff to advance in their career.
- ✓ Talent management allows organizations to make systematic decisions about the development of staff. Employees feel more engaged when they recognize an equitable procedure for advancement.
- ✓ Talent management allows organizations to focus on excellence.

Talent management is a philosophy that must be owned by everyone in the organization, especially senior leadership. Finding and developing talent is the key to sustainable success. At times talent management can appear in conflict with traditional human resources. Practices of consistency can work against finding, retaining, and developing talent. However, if you use integrated thinking, you can still maintain the human resource practices required to remove liability and ensure that some consistent practices are implemented.

For example, a common human resources practice is to have all interviewers ask the same questions to all candidates for fairness. Unfortunately, if the standard questions do not go deep into a candidate's leadership style or how they achieved a result for students, the human resources panel will not know enough about the person's leadership style to make sure they have the skills and abilities to do the job effectively. As one senior human resources leader once said to me, "We hire people for their experience and background and fire them for who they are" (Kirtman, 2014, p. 31). He was saying that we need to find out more information on who the person is, or we may find that they are not the right person for the job after they are hired.

Liability is important but it can conflict with achieving results. As one lawyer told me, "Don't ask a lawyer if you can do something that is different from the standard process. If you ask the lawyer, the answer will be no. You need to say, 'This is the result I want to achieve, and it is different from the rules.' Ask how it can be done legally, and any good lawyer can help you." Great lawyers are not trying to follow the law; they are trying to help their clients within the law. It is not either/or—we can achieve our results and protect ourselves from grievances or lawsuits at the same time.

An example of how a common human resource process can compromise results is the established practice of responding to a complaint about a hostile work environment by a staff member in a school. The unfortunate aspect of a hostile work environment complaint is the lack of focus on the practices that led to the complaint. In addition, the negative aspects of the formal complaint can result in the loss of valued employees and tensions in a department or a team.

The following is an example of how the legal aspect of this kind of complaint and the retaining of talent can be managed together to an effective result. The process outlined is a real-life situation that required integrative thinking and a focus on the North Star, not only the legal compliance process.

HUMAN RESOURCE COMPLIANCE/HOSTILE WORK ENVIRONMENT AND TALENT MANAGEMENT PLUS RETENTION OF STAFF

A staff member in a technology department in a school district in the Midwest sent an email to the human resources department to file a hostile work environment complaint against her supervisor. She felt their supervisor yelled at and humiliated her in front of her team and that whereas previous coaching for her and her supervisor had been effective, this hostile behavior was still occurring. She wanted it to stop and couldn't see any other way but to make a hostile work environment complaint. The superintendent wanted to resolve the problem and didn't want to lose either staff person because of their value to the department and the district. Based on my consultation of how to use integrative thinking to resolve the problem, while preceding legally to prevent any liability concerns, he decided to use the following process.

Consult the Legal Team

First, he spoke to the attorney for the district to explain the process he wanted to follow and to make sure that what he did was legal. The attorney stated that his second step should be to talk to the complainant, and he should confirm her right to file a formal complaint. The lawyer said the superintendent could proceed but had to make sure that the person with the complaint understood that she could file the complaint. If the complainant at any point said she wanted to make a formal complaint, the conversation would stop, and the formal process would proceed.

Meet With the Complainant

The superintendent set up a time for a conversation with the staff member who had the complaint. He asked her to explain what happened and why she was upset. When discussing her concerns, he asked if she would like to look at a mediation and coaching approach with clear outcomes. I was the mediator and coach and worked with both parties. The person with the complaint was willing to proceed with mediation and coaching and agreed to drop the formal complaint. The superintendent asked her again if this was what she wanted to do, and she agreed. The complainant wanted a resolution and was not driven to do anything to hurt her supervisor.

A concern about compliance and how it could block the solving of a problem occurred in this situation. After human resources received an email from the complainant, they told her that an email was not sufficient and that she had to fill out a form for a complaint. If human resources had engaged the kind of integrated thinking the superintendent used, the complaint probably would never have been filed.

Try a Talent Management Approach

The result of the talent management approach in this case was that coaching and mediation were successful. There was an agreement about how the people would work together. The supervisor worked on her skills on how to raise performance issues respectfully and coach her staff to success. The complainant is now comfortable with being a direct report of the director of the department, rather than the supervisor, to improve her performance. The goal is for them to work together when both parties are comfortable.

The formal process may have resulted in the supervisor leaving or feeling attacked. The tension between the two parties would have been palpable and affected the entire department. A talent management approach resulted in the retaining and developing of two talented people in key roles.

Step 2: Develop a Plan for Recruiting and Retaining

As noted in our research (see Chapter 1), we need a workforce that is results oriented, innovative, flexible, persistent, and analytical. In the past, the emphasis was more on experience and less on skills and competencies. We need to pivot to recruiting people with the skills (and developing those skills) that will help students succeed.

RECRUITING STAFF

I have led more than 150 superintendent searches and hundreds of searches for principals and administrators. I have found success by recruiting from my existing network to find talented people. Here are a few of the reasons why recruitment works:

1. Talented people tend to refer other talented people.
2. Although advertising can be effective, recruitment requires going to where the people are by using a network of contacts (this is why the role of influencers today has grown in the business world).
3. People tend to trust people they know.

Recruitment applies to every position and involves identifying talented people in the positions they are in now. Recruitment also applies to finding a diverse workforce. Our data show that the behaviors we are looking for today are strong in women, people of color, and younger people. It may not be obvious from responses to advertisements whether people have the requisite skills we need. In fact, the low number of candidates for most positions tends to force districts to hire a warm body to fill a position. If one recruits through a network of people, potential candidates can be identified more easily. If you focus on talent acquisition and network with talented people, they will recommend other talented people. Being creative and recruiting the best will attract people who want to be on "dream teams." We need to find nontraditional ways of finding candidates. Starting with a plan for recruitment and retention from the beginning of the hiring process is talent management.

SAMPLE EDUCATIONAL HIRING RECRUITMENT WORKSHEET

1. **Position Details**
   - **Position Title:** Special Education Coordinator
   - **Department/School:** Lincoln Elementary School
   - **Full Time/Part Time:** Full Time
   - **Start Date:** August 1, 2025
   - **Salary Range:** $70,000-$85,000
2. **Desired Qualifications**
   - **Minimum Education Level:** Master's Degree in Special Education
   - **Years of Experience:** 5+ years in special education
   - **Special Certifications/Endorsements:** Special Education Certification
   - **Skills Required:**
     - Strong leadership and organizational skills
     - Excellent communication and collaboration abilities
     - In-depth knowledge of special education laws and regulations
     - Experience with IEP development and implementation
   - **Preferred Qualifications:**
     - Previous experience as a special education coordinator
     - Knowledge of assistive technologies
     - Bilingual (Spanish-English)
3. **Target Demographics**
   - **Geographic Location:** Midwest Region
   - **Experience Level:** Mid to Senior Level
   - **Field of Expertise:** Special Education
   - **Diversity Goals:** To increase bilingual and culturally diverse staff
4. **Recruitment Channels**
   - **Job Boards and Websites:**
     - ☑ Indeed
     - ☑ Glassdoor
     - ☑ LinkedIn

(Continued)

(Continued)

- ☐ HigherEdJobs
- ☐ SchoolSpring
- ☐ Other: ____________________

- Professional Organizations:
  - ☑ National Education Association (NEA)
  - ☐ American Association of School Administrators (AASA)
  - ☑ Council for Exceptional Children (CEC)
  - ☐ Other: ____________________
- University Career Centers:
  - ☑ Local Universities
  - ☐ Regional Universities
  - ☐ National Universities
  - ☐ Specific Programs/Departments: ____________________
- Social Media:
  - ☑ Facebook
  - ☑ Twitter
  - ☐ Instagram
  - ☐ Other: ____________________
- Networking Events:
  - ☐ Job Fairs
  - ☑ Education Conferences
  - ☐ Alumni Events
  - ☐ Other: ____________________
- Internal Recruitment:
  - ☑ Promote Within
  - ☑ Employee Referral Program
  - ☐ Internal Job Posting
  - ☐ Other: ____________________

5. **Recruitment Plan**

- Sourcing:
  - Use professional network to identify talented people and ask them to refer.
- Where are the people that we want to attract?
  - Identify locations, organizations, and platforms where desired candidates are active.
- Identify people who have large networks, and ask them to refer:
  - Leverage influencers, community leaders, and professionals with extensive connections.
- Ask talented people who have worked in your district to refer candidates:
  - Reach out to former employees and trusted individuals for recommendations.

6. **Follow-Up Plan**

- Onboarding Process:
  - Orientation Program: Two-day comprehensive orientation program covering district policies, school culture, and specific role responsibilities
  - Mentorship Opportunities: Pairing with a senior special education coordinator for mentorship and support
  - Initial Training: One-week intensive training on IEP development, assistive technologies, and compliance with special education laws
- Retention Strategies:
  - Professional Development: Regular workshops and conferences on special education trends and best practices
  - Quarterly "Fit" Conversations: Assess employee satisfaction and performance and growth goals
  - Career Advancement Opportunities: Clear pathways for career progression within the district's administrative roles
  - Employee Engagement Initiatives: Monthly team-building activities and recognition programs for outstanding performance

This worksheet can be adapted to fit specific needs and requirements of the hiring process. It can also be digitized for ease of use and better tracking.

THINGS TO REMEMBER WHEN PRACTICING TALENT MANAGEMENT

- ✓ Reduce the time and the cost on traditional advertisements that do not attract qualified candidates.
- ✓ Identify internal and external people who have strong networks.
- ✓ Hire a recruiter for hard-to-find positions.
- ✓ Reduce paperwork to apply—only a cover letter and résumé are needed.
- ✓ Eliminate letters of reference—ask for a list of references.
- ✓ Use leadership assessments for finalists to help develop interview questions and references questions based on the assessment's results.
- ✓ Use your network to obtain in-depth references.
- ✓ Job descriptions are limited in value—move toward a portfolio of work.

THINGS TO REMEMBER WHEN PLANNING INTERVIEWS

- ✓ Interview five to eight semifinalists.
- ✓ Interview three to four finalists.
- ✓ Use leadership assessments on three to four finalists.
- ✓ Reduce standard questions to five maximum.
- ✓ Use leadership assessments to ask additional questions.
- ✓ Include follow-up questions.
- ✓ Use résumé-specific questions.
- ✓ Conduct conversational interviews (not overly prescribed or structured).

RECRUITMENT—YOUR ENEMY MAY BE THE BEST HIRE

Christy Allen, a director of special education in Modesto, California, needed a skilled coordinator for her department. She decided to try to recruit. She thought about the attorney who had been her adversary in special education cases for ten years. She had developed a positive working relationship with him over time. So why not try to recruit him? She asked him to apply for the position. He was surprised at first. This would mean leaving his private practice and coming over to the "dark" side to work for the district he had battled on cases for years. He loved working with Christy and decided to apply. Now Modesto has a skilled leader who was also an attorney. He knew the weaknesses that caused them to lose in past cases and how to help them improve. He was asked if he would ever have applied to an advertisement for the position. He answered no and said it was because of his work and respect for Christy that he applied.

The typical approach in most districts is to form hiring committees to screen and interview candidates to recommend by ranking. When we move to a talent management approach, the structure needs to change. If we recruit talented people, they need to have a priority over the process. The process is important, but a results orientation means that we must hire talent. According to Roger L. Martin (2002), "Feeling special is more important to talent than compensation is . . . you must treat them as valued, unique individuals. Never dismiss their ideas, never allow their progress to be blocked, and never miss the chance to shower them with praise when they succeed." Martin illustrated this concept by telling the following story:

> Sometimes that required you to battle the human resource function, which tends to want to treat people homogeneously and limit opportunities to rigid timeframes. I recall getting intense pushback from the head of Monitor when I wanted to assign a less seasoned consultant to a senior role on a major case. I was told he wasn't ready and that it wasn't fair to others who had been at the firm longer. I offered to look for opportunities in the future for those I bypassed and promised to take full responsibility for cleaning up any mess

that resulted from promoting the consultant. Fortunately, it worked out well and catapulted him into a position that eliminated all questions about his readiness. (Martin 2022)

Therefore, the process of hiring talent needs to be different. The hiring committee needs to be advisory only. They can review candidates and present their viewpoints on fit for the district or school. The rankings should not be forwarded because each person may not have the full knowledge of what skills are needed. Too often the best interviewer and nicest person gets hired. Although personality and interviewing skills are important, they are not always the best measurement in hiring.

THE INTERVIEW DOES NOT ALWAYS TELL THE RIGHT STORY

In a superintendent search, a candidate for the position who had a financial management background made a potentially fatal mistake in his public interview. When asked what his vision was for the district, he replied, "You mean on facilities?" He was totally flustered. As the search firm consultant, I realized that this excellent leader made a mistake that could result in him being eliminated. He had excellent skills as a leader; I knew he would be a high-performing superintendent who would have a successful career.

The school board said we had no choice but to eliminate him. I explained that he had the skills they needed and that our leadership assessments confirmed my viewpoint. I suggested that they provide another chance by altering the process. Because the role required interactions with a range of community groups, parents, and municipal leaders, we added a set of meetings and interviews. for all three of the finalists. The school board agreed, and the candidates completed their interviews. The data were overwhelming that the candidate who made the almost fatal mistake in his interview was their candidate of choice. He was hired unanimously and has been one of the best superintendents in the state for more than fifteen years.

RETAINING STAFF

Now that we have expanded our pool of candidates, we need to retain and develop our talent. The concept of fit discussions is often the key to retention in other sectors that focus on talent management. Talent management is about fit: fit with the culture and environment, fit with use of a person's strengths, and fit with work-life balance (see Figure 4.2). What fits someone when they are hired may not fit them a year later. We have noticed that fit discussions have a major effect on people because they may be struggling with personal issues, a difficult boss or other issues. If these issues are not discussed, then that person could leave suddenly.

4.2 Talent Management Fit Factors

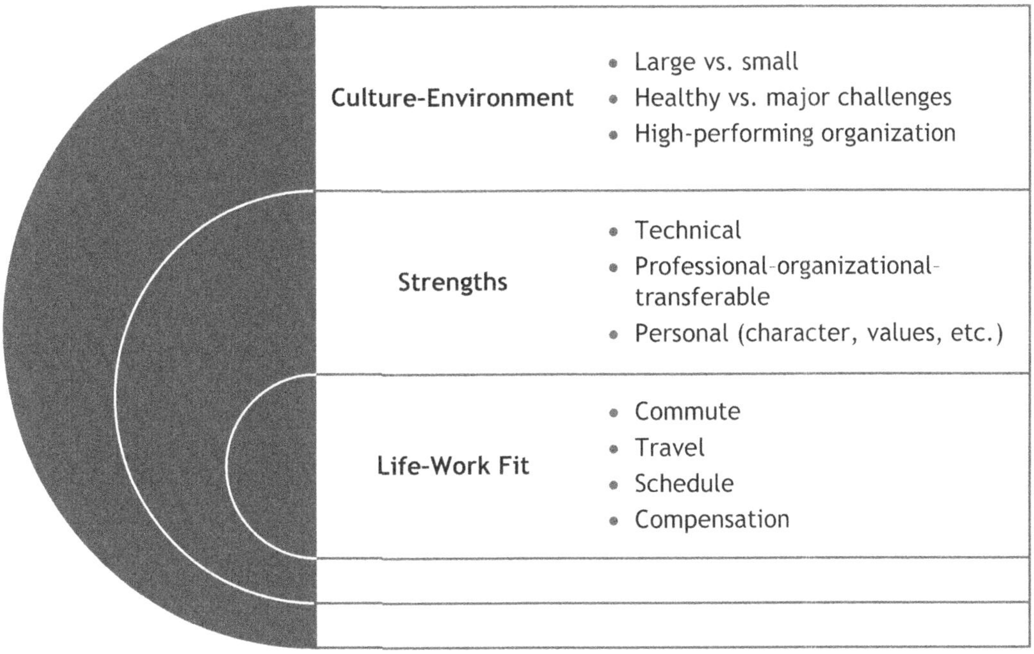

Environmental Fit

One aspect of a fit conversation discusses the environment that the employee wants to work in and why.

- ✓ Does the person want to work in an urban district to provide needed services to disadvantaged communities?
- ✓ Does the person want to work in a rural district because they grew up in a rural community and did not see enough services to help students succeed?

- ✓ Does the person want to work in a small district to have variety in their work, or does a suburban district providing more resources motivate them to achieve?
- ✓ Does the person want to deal with conflict and help solve problems, or do they want a high-performing district to work on higher level skills for students and staff?

Strengths Fit

Fit conversations need to understand and build on people's strengths. A strength equals something you are both good at and like to do.

- ✓ Does the person have strong instructional skills?
- ✓ Is the person great at motiving people?
- ✓ Do the values of the person connect well to the values of the district?
- ✓ Is the person creative and would like to have opportunities to use their creativity?

Life/Work Fit

A growing aspect of fit is life-work balance.

- ✓ Is the commute time too long?
- ✓ Can the person have flexibility to deal with childcare?
- ✓ Is the compensation fair, what benefits interest them the most, and what is missing that would meet their needs?
- ✓ Are there many evening meetings that could put a strain on their home life?

RETENTION: LOOKING TO STAY BUT MAY HAVE TO LEAVE

A principal has been successful leading a virtual academy for two years. She has improved her Workplace Personality Inventory (WPI) scores on achievement orientation, innovation, and analytical thinking. Her high concern for others has been a barrier and led to her getting overwhelmed by too many tasks. Unfortunately, a recent death in her family had forced her to change her priorities. She needed much more flexibility in her schedule to take care of family issues or more salary to pay for help. She felt a job with the state department of education was the answer.

The fit for quality of life would work better in a state position. However, her increased skills as a leader and love for innovation would not be used as well in a state position that might be narrower or compliance driven. Additionally, her fit for the culture of the school and her job work well in her current role.

A fit conversation with her supervisor provided an important and useful forum. The principal wanted to stay but would need more flexibility or an increase in salary to hire help to meet the needs of her personal life. The supervisor re-confirmed the district's commitment to her talent and provided both more flexibility and an increase in salary. She now feels invigorated. In addition, she has been told she needs to delegate more and worry less about burdening her staff. This will positively affect her high concern for others and lower stress tolerance scores in her WPI. Her personal situation forced her to delegate and was a great opportunity for the supervisor to coach her on delegation. The great news is the staff stepped up and helped the principal in so many ways. Now the principal is excited about building the program and adding new innovations.

The focus on academic success based on the Portrait of the Graduate is the center of every fit discussion. In these discussions the leader should delve into how the culture of the district or school applies to the staff member. The integration of social emotional learning (SEL), equity, and academics discussed in Chapter 3 also works for staff. A person dealing with a sick parent (SEL) will have different challenges than someone who may feel disconnected from their colleagues based on experience, race, age, or other factors (equity). We have learned from our discussions on our leadership assessment data that people of color have rarely had genuine conversations about equity with their supervisor. These conversations should involve a review of scores on achievement orientation, persistence, innovation, analytical thinking, and other key leadership traits then move to how the culture of the school on issues that may be affecting work and motivation. Experiences based on race or gender, for example, may have resulted in a person not feeling valued or supported because they are viewed as challenging the status quo. The result of the conversation on fit might be to find opportunities for the person to be innovative and find new ways to make the curriculum relevant to all students.

If the teacher feels they must follow the curriculum exactly, if they are innovative they can feel stifled. Many teachers have told me they feel they have lost the art of teaching. A teacher who is innovative and encouraged to supplement the curriculum with new ways to connect to students will be more motivated and feel there is a better fit for them in the district.

DEVELOPMENT—STIFLING INNOVATION

A teacher in the Midwest is surprised by her high innovation scores on her WPI. She notes that no one has ever tried to tap into her innovative abilities. She further adds that her ideas are discouraged because they are so different from other teachers. She believes that using opportunities for students to apply learning to real life and personal cultures would make the academics more relevant and engaging. The principal tells her that she needs to follow the curriculum and not distract the students. This talented teacher has been shut down and has lost her desire to take any initiative. She ends up leaving the district to seek opportunities where she could be herself and feel valued.

This scenario is not unique. Many issues can cause potential leaders to feel stifled. Women leaders often report that they have not had conversations with their supervisors about the fact that when they assert leadership, some male staff react negatively or have difficulty working for a woman. Our data have shown that many women of color are highly innovative but have never been recognized or supported for their creativity. Young leaders may struggle with a lack of respect from veteran staff when they assert their leadership. All life experience affects a person's fit in the organization and should be a part of regular conversations.

Fit conversations, which are important in presenting feedback to staff, will uncover these concerns, which then can be addressed in your district's culture and in the skill development. The staff member can review their strengths and what would make them feel fulfilled in their position, and the supervisor can provide feedback on what the staff member can do to improve their effectiveness. Feedback provided during a motivational fit conversation will be more effective than a typical evaluation meeting. The difference is in have goal-setting fit conversation, not an evaluation meeting. The staff member will feel that their supervisor is listening and supporting them. If the meeting's focus is to work together on goals and improvement, critical feedback is better received. Ongoing feedback is not emphasized enough in education. These conversations will be explored more in Chapter 5.

Once the fit conversations happen more frequently, you will see the retention of staff increase. You will also be able to identify talent and open career paths for people who may have not been noticed. This will give you a competitive advantage to find, retain, and develop talent.

Fit conversations are effective in promoting personal and professional conversations for all staff on how they are valued and how their concerns can be discussed in a productive manner However, these individual conversations, although important, do not directly deal with how to develop organizational strategies to increase staff satisfaction.

STEPS FOR HAVING FIT CONVERSATIONS WITH YOUR TEAM

Step 1: Set up a team retreat to focus on a balance between people and academic content work in your school or district. This team can comprise the principal, assistant principals, high-performing teachers, and other support roles.

Step 2: Ask each person to report on a recent fit discussion with their supervisor and fit discussions they have had with their direct reports. Honest fit discussions will help build trust. The Trust Cycle (see Figure 4.3) provides an approach to build trust among people and teams.

Step 3: Each team member should discuss how they can support each other's leadership development.

Step 4: Ask each team member if any of their fit discussions have school or district implications. Gather suggestions on how these implications can or should be addressed.

Step 5: The team provides specific ways to support each member's personal and professional growth and develop an overall goal for the team.

Step 6: Set norms to build trust for genuine team discussions.

4.3 The Trust Cycle

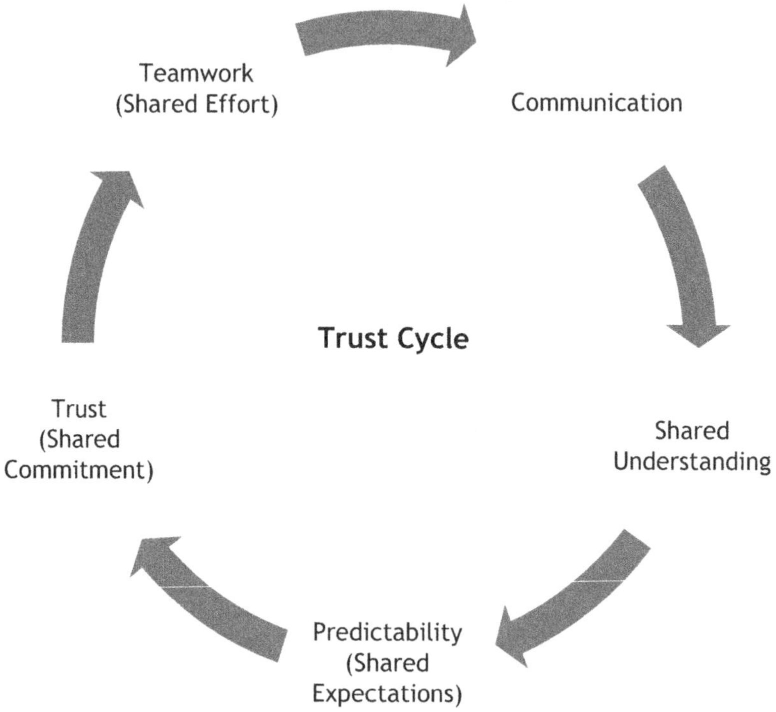

Source: Adapted from the work of Jerry Stinnett

Figure 4.3 illustrates the Trust Cycle. Communication begins in Step 1 which leads to Step 2—a shared understanding. Then dialog can lead to shared expectations (Step 3). At this stage, trust is built on a clear sense of predictable behavior. If this phase is missed, people will still predict behavior, but the predictions may be inaccurate and negative based on a lack of clear expectations, leading to mistrust based on perceived actions. Step 4, the shared commitment phase, involves the distribution of responsibility and accountability to complete tasks or assignments. When commitment is established, people can count on each other to get the work done to complete the task. Commitment is strong at this point because trust is building on a sound base of understanding and expectations that are clear to all parties. The final stage of trust, teamwork (Step 5), is reached based on a team's goals developed in a safe and trusting environment. A team cannot be formed simply by throwing people into a room and giving them a project (Kirtman, 2014).

Trust is always the elephant in the room regarding retention. If people feel a lack of trust, it is difficult to improve the culture and provide an environment for staff to be successful and make a difference for students. Patrick Lencioni (2005) in his book, *Overcoming the Five Dysfunctions of a Team*, lists trust as the basic building block to move toward results. A team has to be able to have one-on-one fit discussions to build trust with their supervisor and then build into team discussions that allow people to be genuine without fear of repercussions. Trust is the topic of many team and leadership books. It is hard to develop and so easy to lose. Trust is not a linear process; teams need to work on trust and test it by taking on difficult challenges.

In his overview of *Overcoming the Five Dysfunctions of a Team*, Lencioni (2005) wrote, "The true measure of a team is that it accomplishes the results it sets out to achieve. To do that on a consistent, ongoing basis, a team must overcome the five dysfunctions" (p. 80). Using the framework of the five disfunctions of a team (and its corresponding high-performance team behaviors), a district or school team can begin to have in-depth and effective fit conversations.

LENCIONI'S FIVE DISFUNCTIONS OF A TEAM

1. Absence of trust versus building trust
2. Fear of conflict verses mastering conflict
3. Lack of commitment versus achieving commitment
4. Avoidance of accountability versus embracing accountability
5. Inattention to results versus focusing on results

Step 3: Building Sustainable Leadership Through Talent Development

Talent development is critical to retention and improving results for students. When a school or district sets high expectations for student results, the quality of staff is paramount. All staff benefit from development, and a plan for building the capacity of all staff needs the highest attention.

The first step to directly managing the workforce crisis is to focus on teacher leadership. Relying on the people who are closest to the students is a high-impact strategy. Real teacher leadership is well beyond having teachers volunteer for committees. Teacher leadership needs to have two integrated areas of focus:

- Instructional leadership
- Organizational leadership

Most teacher leadership programs focus on instruction and content only. This focus is too narrow to ensure sustainable results for students and retention of quality teachers. Teachers often tell me that their certification program focuses only on the students. There is virtually no focus on working with adults. One teacher stated to me, "I only know how to work with students and have no strategies for dealing with adults. I try to use the same techniques with the adults, and they rarely work."

Because certification programs don't usually prepare teachers to work with parents, colleagues, central office staff, or other adults in the building and the district, teachers may become frustrated and stressed. Dealing with a difficult parent, talking to a principal who is overly compliance oriented or not coaching teachers, or understanding how financial resources are allocated are all relevant topics teachers are not exposed to in training programs.

Many district leaders complain that the only way to engage with teachers on change is through the unions. The best approach to improving results is to help teachers be leaders in the classroom, the school, and the district. This means that district leadership genuinely needs to seek out and listen to teachers' voices.

Leaders often complain that teachers do not understand the finances, politics, and stresses of being an administrator. Part of the reason for this lack of understanding of the big picture is that teachers are sheltered by leaders to ensure they are not distracted from teaching.

This is an outdated viewpoint that doesn't work today. Teachers need to be seen as professionals and learn how to be effective teachers *and* leaders. It is next to impossible to shelter teachers in today's world of social media. We need to be engaged with teachers to help them act as professionals. This will require giving up some control to teachers to make informed decisions about students.

Teacher leadership is a key effort that involves all aspects of talent management. Recruiting the best teachers and focusing on retention and development must be priorities in every district to improve student achievement. The North Star will provide the focus for teachers. The district must practice the philosophy that teachers need to be valued and have a voice. Teachers also need to be able to make decisions without bureaucracy that affects students' success.

We need to shift from antiquated philosophies such as this: "Teacher leadership is like letting the inmates run the asylum." The prevailing attitude in education has been that teachers are the problem and need to be told what to do. We need to change our attitudes toward teachers. They have difficult jobs, especially during these challenging times when they are pulled away from their focus on students for far too many initiatives. The Portrait of the Graduate will allow teachers to be unified in what success means for their students.

CREATING A TEACHER LEADER PROGRAM THAT WILL MAKE A DIFFERENCE

One district was able to promote 20 percent of its teachers to leadership positions within one year in the heart of the workforce crisis. Additionally, other teachers in the program reported that they were feeling their voices were being heard and were excited about staying in the district. In fact, one teacher, a union president, stated in a public meeting that she wished all teachers could be part of their teacher leader program.

The following are steps that a district can follow to form an effective teacher leader program.

A district should ask for teacher volunteers or nominations from principals to join the program. It is recommended that the superintendent lead at least two of these sessions to develop a direct relationship with the teachers. The ground rules of this group are to listen and learn, not judge the principal or any other leaders or colleagues. Topics such as data analysis, financial or budget concerns, community involvement and partnerships, and so on can be included. In several programs union leadership can participate to increase their leadership skills because they have a high impact on results. Central office leaders could also lead sessions as part of the program. These sessions are generally two hours long but can vary depending on each district's schedule.

THE GENERAL OUTLINE OF A TEACHER LEADER PROGRAM

Session 1: What does teacher leadership mean?

Session 2: Know yourself—understanding each teachers' leadership profile.

Session 3: Build teachers skills in both instruction and organization.

Session 4: Apply new leadership skills to your school leadership team and your Classroom.

Session 5: What are your goals for leadership development, and how can school and district leadership support your growth?

Being personally involved in starting several teacher leadership programs has been rewarding for me. Teachers are hungry to learn and be treated as professionals. The added benefit of these programs is that the learning is applied immediately into the classroom without any bureaucracy or delays. The program allows superintendents to know firsthand how the work in the district directly affects teaching and learning. Whether it is a small or large district, the on-the-ground knowledge at the point of connection to the student is invaluable to leadership.

Step 4: Integrate the Components of Talent Management

Districts tend to have different departments and people involved in separate components of talent management or human resources. If we establish that each administrator should integrate the following functions listed into their work, the employees will feel more valued, and the retention of talent will increase.

In recruiting a new teacher, the principal and their potential colleagues will probably be more motivational than a human resource person. Although human resources can reach out to potential candidates, the principal or another teacher would probably be better at closing the deal to have a talented teacher join the team. If a superintendent does not directly discuss salary and benefits with a new administrator (because HR handles all salary issues), then they are missing an opportunity to understand how the new person feels about the job. Are they settling for now and planning to leave when they find what they really want, or are they interested in a different role but could not find a position? This is especially important information for retention. If the hiring person discusses salary and benefits, the vision and mission of the district, the culture and community, and professional development, they can increase retention and development of staff. When these functions are managed by different departments, perhaps for efficiency reasons, it can have an adverse effect on the retention of talent.

According to Mark Mortensen and Amy C. Edmondson (2023) in today's world of hiring and retaining, we need a new "employee value proposition." An employee value proposition is "a system composed of four interrelated factors," which include the following:

1. Materials offerings—salary and benefit offerings
2. Opportunities to develop and grow
3. Connection and community
4. Meaning and purpose

"An effective and enduring employee value proposition requires treating the four factors as independent parts of an integrative system" (Mortensen & Edmondson, 2023, p. 7). What follows is some guidance as to how this employee value proposition can be implemented in education.

FACTOR 1: SALARY AND BENEFITS

It is typical in education for human resources to deal with all salary and benefits because there may be pay scales with contracts and little ability to adjust. The professional growth work is usually through professional development and is less individualized. In some districts there are opportunities to attend conferences or training programs, but they may not be directly tied to the work in the classroom. Teachers who attend professional development should be encouraged to bring back what they've learned, integrate it into their practice, and share their learnings with other faculty. In addition, they need to address how the professional development will improve student learning. The growth and development work is minimal in the classified area because they are not considered to be professionals. Other industries use staff development and do not distinguish professionals from classified personnel as critical for success. This distinction can result in classified staff feeling they are second class. If a supervisor has a conversation about compensation with any employee, regardless of the contract and pay scale, they can observe the commitment and career aspirations of the employee. This information can help find opportunities for advancement for the person.

FACTOR 2: OPPORTUNITIES TO DEVELOP AND GROW

In fit conversations, areas for growth and development can be established in a collaborative manner. The supervisor can then follow up with the employee about what they have learned and how they can apply any instructional and/or organizational training as well as receive coaching and support for their growth and development.

FACTOR 3: CONNECTION AND COMMUNITY

Connection to the internal and external community is not often a stated goal for staff unless their job requires the connection. The seventh competency in Kirtman's Seven Competencies for High-Performing Leaders (Kirtman, 2014) is to build networks and partnerships. This tends to be minimized in most districts unless the role of the leader has a direct connection to the community. However, connecting to the community should be part of every person's role. The commitment to the organization and retention will increase if staff feel part of the community.

FACTOR 4: MEANING AND PURPOSE

The meaning and purpose of the district and school are often an aspect of leadership retreats and documents on values, vision, or strategic plans but not usually tied to the other components of the employee experience on a regular basis. Determining how an employee feels about the mission and values is important to motivation. Too often people in districts believe the values are on paper but not modeled by leadership. Discussing the meaning of the work for each employee and the organizational values is an important area for employee commitment and retention. Educators chose their field to make a difference and advance the values that they believe are important. It is critical to build this aspect into their work. It can also mean that employees that conflict with the vision and values of the organization may not be a good fit moving forward. An example of this not being a fit was a member of a maintenance team in an urban district where values were openly discussed. One maintenance supervisor expressed his concern that students were not being punished enough for negative behavior and that the district's move toward restorative justice was a joke. This maintenance supervisor was spreading this opinion internally and driving some staff away because he would confront them. This staff member was encouraged to find another job.

CHAPTER SUMMARY

The workforce crisis is affecting every industry. Since the pandemic, employees are looking at their work contracts differently. Employees want flexible schedules to focus more on quality of life; they are not choosing jobs based only on salary but are now considering other factors such as their voice being heard, safety, and opportunities for growth and learning. The traditional methods of hiring are not working. The number and quality of candidates for important positions are slim. Education is having the same problems as other industries but is not pivoting n to solve or at least mitigate the workforce crisis.

This chapter provided an approach to change this narrative and find and keep talented staff to increase student achievement. Evolving human resources to talent management provides new tools and methods to find and keep talent. Focusing on a strategy that integrates recruitment, retention, and development of all staff is essential. Developing teachers as leaders of instruction and organizational change is paramount. The teachers are the closest to the students, and if equipped with new tools and a voice that is valued, they will improve student achievement.

Leaders need to change their definition of leadership from command and control to developing the capacity to lead others through a culture of coaching for results. If we do not change, we will see the migration of talent away from education to other sectors that have pivoted their leadership.

CHAPTER TAKEAWAYS

- Focus human resources on talent management, and develop a comprehensive strategy based on the current needs of students and the workforce.
- Develop a recruitment and retention strategy (develop a culture for people of color to attract and retain).

(Continued)

(Continued)

- Redesign your organizational chart to focus on results and leadership, not tasks and processes (overuse of coordinator, compliance, and support titles).
- Don't only ask teachers why they are leaving; ask why they are staying (connection and voice).
- Focus on developing teacher leadership in your teaching staff to improve teacher retention.
- Implement systems where supervisors routinely check for fit among all staff and where staff routinely self-assess whether the school is meeting the
- Use fit discu
- Use your tal
job. Don't w
might lose tl
- Create a cul
serve as lea
- Use leaderst
developmen

QUESTIONS FOR REFLECTION

1. How can you identify talented people in your district without looking only at titles?
2. What are key positions that do not have the quality and/or quantity of candidates that you need? How can you build a recruitment strategy to fill these positions with talented people?
3. How can you think of the teachers as drivers to improve student achievement?
4. Are leaders in the district working on their leadership and practicing every day for improvement? If not, how can you build leadership development into the work with every staff member?
5. How can your present talent management to obtain buy-in for needed change to deal with the workforce crisis in your district?

5

SETTING HIGH EXPECTATIONS FOR ALL STUDENTS AND STAFF

Learning Intentions

1. Learn how to establish a high expectations culture for all students, staff, school board, parents, and community in a district.
2. Understand the Indigo assessment data on students and staff and how it affects high expectations.
3. Understand how high expectations contribute to student success.

What Is the Problem We Are Trying to Solve?

Every district leader says they have high standards for students and staff. However, saying that and doing it consistently is difficult. High expectations must be an integral part of the overall culture of a district. The school board, parents, teachers, and administrators need to commit to creating and maintaining the culture for the results to occur as defined by the Portrait of the Graduate. If the students are surrounded by adults who are on the same page and expect excellence, they will achieve and feel supported in their goals. This must be infectious to include support roles, athletics, municipal government, and every constituency that touches education and the lives of students.

Unfortunately, as leaders have become more task driven, the focus on high expectations for students and staff has declined. School boards and other groups have slipped into their tasks and agendas and lost track of their North Star. Educators can become caught up in the weeds of compliance requirements that erode focus on high expectations. As Peter DeWitt (2022b) said, "Too often, the required actions leaders must accomplish from year to year become acts of compliance." In addition, lack of clarity on what student achievement means (see Chapter 3) has contributed to myriads of tasks blur the focus on results. The pandemic also accelerated the lowering of standards for academic excellence and performance. The focus on social and emotional (SEL) issues, although important to address the increase of stress and mental health issues for both staff and students, has resulted in some districts emphasizing SEL over academics.

Some educators fear that having high expectations for staff will cause them to leave their district. Others believe that high expectations are not fair for students or staff because of increasing stress and mental health issues that are affecting everyone.

Many districts fear failure and are afraid to make mistakes, which results in lowering standards for everyone. At the same time every district says that they have high expectations of all teachers and staff. The most effective administrator sees the best in people and brings forth excellence for everyone to learn from each other: the teacher who connects to their students and never lowers expectations no matter what and the custodian who takes pride in the school and connects every day to the students.

Although these fears are understandable, leaders who believe in their people, do not compromise on high standards, and build the capacity of all staff to manage their stress better will attract people to be a part of their successful venture. As one Latina leader from a district that is 80% Latino in students and staff, said to me, "We too often use the expression in Spanish *poor mijo* (poor child)." Setting lower expectations is contagious, but setting high expectations to meet today's challenges and succeed is even more contagious.

A major aspect of low expectations is that people do not provide direct feedback to staff or each other. One can be direct in feedback and still supportive of the person's growth (integrative thinking). Educators struggle to be direct with each other. The concern for others score on the Workplace Personality Inventory (WPI) for teachers, noted in Chapter 1 and in Appendix F, is too high. The fear can be that if a teacher becomes upset, they will quit, and it is hard to find someone to fill their spot. The resulting lack of the ability to provide direct feedback has an effect on high expectations. If a person does not know what they are doing well or what needs to improve, how will they improve their craft? In districts where I work, I coach leaders and teachers to be direct with each other by modeling that behavior. Most leaders will say they encourage people to have direct conversations with colleagues, parents, administrators, and support staff. However, in most cases people do not have the conversations they need to have. I've taken on the role to push these conversations to occur to break the culture of indirect conversations. I typically identify a common problem that is happening in a school and ask the principal to ask a colleague for assistance. I then follow up to see if the conversation happened. I coach the leaders at all levels to use this same practice.

Unfortunately, not only is this difficult to implement, but I also receive feedback that that this process breaks confidentiality and promotes gossip. This criticism arises because people become uncomfortable and do not allow private conversations that need to be more open to occur.

As one prominent leader said that she has improved as a leader based on a situation where she was complaining about a person to me. I stopped our conversation and asked that person to join us. There was no blame or conflict, only a direct, honest, and nonjudgmental conversation. Now this leader is much more direct with people to everyone's benefit.

Gossip involves secret comments about things that are not true. I show leaders how I take the truth, as one person sees it, and make sure it is discussed. If I talk to someone about a truth regarding another person, I immediately call that other person and tell them about the conversation. Once each person's truth is discussed directly, it can often be resolved quickly; most situations tend to be misunderstandings and not real conflicts.

It is interesting that in the last five years I have been working with teachers, using the same process, and I have not received any complaints. The complaints come from principals and administrators. Teachers tend to be more open to honest conversations and learning how to improve their leadership.

Too often I see administrators assuming how teachers feel without knowing the truth. Unfortunately, when administrators ask teachers, teachers often hold back on what they believe. Once organizations stop making assumptions and have direct conversations with colleagues, we can move ahead to results. When educators do not have to worry about repercussions from expressing how they feel, direct, honest, and productive conversations can ensue. Educators who are honest with each other and assume positive intent can build high-performance cultures.

However, high performers with the courage to provide direct, honest feedback or challenge the status quo can hit barriers and receive criticism from people who are not willing to be truthful or take risks. Resistance can cause the high performer to pull back from being open and honest to fit into the current culture. In New England, John Pierce (personal communication, 2024), a former high school principal and leadership coach, said that having courage to speak the truth is like crabs in a bucket. When there are several crabs in a bucket, and one tries to crawl out, the other crabs pull them back in. When successful people in a district speak up or demonstrate innovation and success, we often try to pull them back.

This dynamic of setting high expectations and creating a culture of excellence occurs in other sectors too. Andrew Flanagan (personal communication, 2024), town manager in Andover, Massachusetts, is not like most town managers, who typically are about maintaining the status quo. Flanagan became town manager at the age of thirty, which is very unusual. He was bold, visionary, and driven to make Andover the top destination community north of Boston. He set high expectations for himself and the people around him. Being open and honest with his leadership team and committed to building leadership skills for all staff, accomplished many results that most managers would not have even tried to achieve. Flanagan has been criticized by some for not doing things the way they have always been done, for example, in his approach to recruiting and retaining talented people by offering access to affordable childcare options and flexible schedules rather than reinforcing expectations of lower pay with the goal of retiring and receiving a pension. Understanding that young candidates wanted something different, Flanagan attracted people from other communities and from the private sector who would never have considered working in town government. He did not let the crabs pull him back into the bucket. Brittney Lavoie, a successful former principal, now heads up Flanagan's talent management and human resource office even though she has to human resources background. Lavoie is another example of finding talent in places you would not normally look.

Providing safe places for venting relieves stress and creates a culture that promotes problem-solving and positive results. Unfortunately, this doesn't happen often. In addition, people who score high in concern for others in our leadership assessments end up as receptacles for venting. This can cause more stress for the receiver and make it difficult to act for fear of breaking confidentiality. People who score high on concern for others in the WPI can become overinvolved emotionally, which can have a negative effect on their productivity.

How do we change the culture to promote high expectations and help people support and learn from each other? This is a simple concept but so hard to accomplish.

What Is Our Proposed Solution?

Standards need to stay high all the time for students, staff, and all other constituents. Although it is commonly stated in many educational circles that learning losses were extreme during the pandemic, several teachers maintained high standards by integrating SEL, equity or DEI, and academics, which resulted in increases in student achievement. Here is one example:

> Though I've always integrated social-emotional learning support into my teaching, the pandemic's impact has forced me to make it even more central to my classroom practice. This change has not only had a major positive impact on my students—and my own—well-being, but it has also resulted in the creation of a more effective learning environment. (Ferlazzo, 2022)

This shows that students and staff can thrive in a high expectations culture no matter what barriers they face.

Set High Expectations

Indigo Education Company, founded by Sheri Smith, and Target Training International (Indigo's technology partner) wanted to research the question "Is there an average student?" Based on more than 15,000 students across multiple states, representing many demographics and academic performance levels, there was not one student who was "average." This study looked at ten dimensions from the Indigo Assessment and looked at the average of each of these dimensions (the middle 30%). "Out of 15,012 students, not one fell into the average of even 9 out of the 10 categories. Even more surprising, less than 2% of the students were average after the first four dimensions" (Smith, 2018). Because there really are no average students, we need to understand who students are as people. Only then can we individualize our education system to the benefit of each child. Once each student is educated as a whole child, we can prepare them for postsecondary education and life.

Our research on adults gives more context to the importance of high standards for students. Through our partnership with Indigo, we have data that students in general are interested in learning deeply, applying their education to real-life experiences, engaging in innovation, and being successful in life. In fact, students show many of the traits that we want from adult leaders today.

The Indigo data show that students have higher expectations for themselves than many educators may believe. Unfortunately, behavior problems and a discipline focus can affect our belief that students want to succeed. Even the language that we use affects high expectations. A number of districts are beginning to call their students scholars to show that they believe that all students can succeed.

Indigo's results provide more data and approaches to set high expectations for all students. In addition, they are aligned with the leadership research we conducted for adults. The use of the data in this book on students provides additional avenues for the work defined by Universal Design Learning (UDL; CAST, 2018).

UDL has been around for a long time and promotes strategies to meet the needs of all learners. It is built on the principle that all students have diverse strengths and needs. By offering flexible learning paths, UDL allows educators to provide multiple ways for students to engage with content, demonstrate knowledge, and sustain motivation. This approach fosters high expectations in several ways.

UDL FOSTERS HIGH EXPECTATIONS BY . . .

1. **Infusing Equity in Learning Access:** UDL eliminates barriers by providing varied methods for students to interact with materials, which helps all students, including those with disabilities, reach their fullest potential. This access encourages educators to hold the same high expectations for every student, knowing they have support in place.
2. **Focusing on Strengths, Not Limitations:** By allowing students to leverage their strengths (e.g., through alternative ways of demonstrating understanding like projects, presentations, or digital media), UDL supports high standards without being limited to traditional, one-size-fits-all measures of success.
3. **Producing a Growth Mindset and Effort:** UDL promotes a growth mindset by designing challenges that are neither too easy nor too hard but just right for each learner. This balance encourages students to put forth effort and take ownership of their progress, reinforcing high expectations.
4. **Nurtures Self-Regulation and Independence:** Through self-directed learning options and opportunities for self-assessment, UDL empowers students to become aware of their own learning processes. This autonomy and self-regulation reinforce high expectations as students learn to take accountability for their academic growth.

By providing ways for each student to succeed, UDL raises the bar and maintains high standards for all students, making learning both rigorous and achievable. The following are some highlights of the Indigo inventory for students that verify that high expectations are a key to student success.

Student Behavior Trends

- Students are generally results oriented. They want to know why they are being asked to answer a question or the goal of writing an essay. They are looking for how the knowledge they are learning applies to their lives.
- Students thrive on building relationships with other students and potentially with teachers.

- Students are interested in what difference it makes to learn a new concept. They will take the time to learn if it applies to what they believe is interesting or important.
- Students will generally comply with rules but may question them if they do not understand their purpose.

From the Indigo data, students generally value the following:

1. They value learning and are interested in data and depth of learning.
2. They want to know the value of what they are learning and how it applies to their life beyond their formal education. They want to know if there will be a return on investment both of their time and for financial gain.
3. They want to make a difference in the world. They often see value beyond themselves. More girls are committed to making a difference for people in the world.
4. They are willing to raise questions or concerns if something does not make sense to them. They are willing to engage in conflict or express differences of opinion to learn.
5. They want power to express their opinions and to be heard.
6. They are not overly judgmental of other people.

Faculty Behavior Trends

1. They are more focused on tasks and less on outcomes.
2. With their colleagues, they are usually relationship oriented.
3. They are focused on slowing things down to gain consistency and at times to include more people in an activity or process.
4. They generally believe in following rules.

Faculty Values

1. They are interested in learning and believe data is important.
2. They are not as interested in money as a motivator and tend not to be focused on the application of learning.
3. They are committed to making a difference in the world for their students and families.

4. They are not generally interested in power and will defer to people in positional power.
5. They prefer to avoid conflict. They like harmony and can find conflict upsetting.
6. They can be judgmental. This can mean that values such as respect for authority, work ethic, honesty, and other personal values can be key to their work and life.

As one can see there are many differences between the behavior of students and faculty. The values are also significantly different.

The students' behavior and values can be connected to strong adult leaders. Being results oriented, moving quickly to outcomes, and building relationships are all qualities of leaders. The students' values of being interested in learning, having the power to make a difference, making money to be successful, and being less judgmental are again all values of successful leaders.

However, the faculty's behavior of staying on task, following rules, and slowing things down without showing application can and often does disconnect them from their students.

The faculty's values of avoiding conflict can result in feeling their power being threatened by student questions. This can result in faculty seeing students (who may be exerting leadership qualities) as difficult and demonstrating behavior problems, which would require discipline.

In addition, Indigo's data on students of color show similar student trends as white students with even stronger leadership behaviors and values for Black and Hispanic students. Although their behavior and values are like white students', white teachers can have difficulty dealing with students of color when different behaviors and values are apparent.

Not being able to discuss these disconnects between students and faculty can result in too much effort on behavior issues and classroom management and less on how to engage students in learning based on who they are as people.

These data are by no means presented to blame faculty for this disconnect. Faculty behavior and potential values are by-products of the task-oriented, compliant world they live in. As we have discussed, teachers need more voice, training, and support on how to engage their students in learning.

Why are all these data connected to our pivot on high expectations? The disconnect with students outlined here tends to lower the expectations for learning. Teachers are faced with managing a class to decrease conflict. Instead, if teachers had these data and understood how to engage and support all students to raise expectations, we would find that students would succeed at higher levels.

The following vignette is from a teacher who made a specific effort to connect to her students in relation to their values and behaviors.

HOW YOU GET WHAT YOU WANT

Angee Phraxayavong-Briones, a former middle school teacher and current principal at Gateway Community Charters in Sacramento, California, encouraged authentic conversations of pathways for students tied to areas high interest and real-life learning.

In a lesson to engage students on potential career paths, they were tasked to take a career interest survey and create digital vision boards of their dreams for the future. This included where they wanted to live and the type of house, vehicle, careers, interests, and endeavors they wanted to pursue.

In a review of a vision board, a student shared a picture of a large home with six bedrooms and high-end amenities and a luxury vehicle. Low-utilitarian teachers who would say an expensive car or fancy house is not important but, rather, how you can help others is more valuable. Low-utilitarian teachers may insist to high-utilitarian students the teachers' values are more important. This would immediately disengage the student. Instead, Phraxayavong-Briones validated the student's dreams and responded, "Wow, that is a nice car and home! Did you have a chance to look up the cost?" The student did not, and this provided an opportunity for student-to-teacher connection.

Together, Phraxayavong-Briones and the student researched housing prices (similar houses listed at $2.3 million) and vehicle prices (the model pictured listed at $250,000). The question then moved to how the student would pay for the car and house. Phraxayavong-Briones explained that these costs did not include other needs or bills such as food, phone, and more. The student shared that the career test show being a social worker aligned with her interests; she loved to help others. From there, the student's next task was to research the average salary of a social worker and steps needed to obtain a career in that field. As Phraxayavong-Briones moved about the classroom checking in with other students, she heard the student exclaim, "Mrs. Briones! I can't afford anything with my salary, and it's going to take me forever to finish school!" Phraxayavong-Briones responded, "Of course you can afford *something*, and anything worth having takes *time*. But you have to decide: Do you adjust what you want based on your career? Or do you adjust your career to get the life you want? Only you can decide that path."

Rather than shut down the student's vision, Phraxayavong-Briones worked with the student's values and interests. She helped the student control her own plan and choices and see potential challenges. The student was engaged in setting her own path and high expectations. Phraxayavong-Briones was a coach, guide on the student's side.

Indigo's data on students and faculty further indicate the disconnect that can happen in education. Students are ready to learn and be challenged. The teacher could be trained and coached to treat students as potential leaders. Unfortunately, the education system, with its focus on tasks and compliance, prevents teachers from partnering with students and engaging in a learning process that engages them and encourages them to reach for their dreams.

The most frequent concern I hear from faculty is that behavior problems block learning. Indigo's data provide a new theory that the students can and will learn if we engage them in their own learning. In fact, the faculty and administration will be able to set and meet high expectations if they move to a results culture that treats students as though they have high potential. Instead of saying students are at risk, Dr. Victor Rios, professor at University of California, Santa Barbara has said they are "at promise."

Teachers who engage students tend to have fewer behavioral problems. Students, faculty, and staff must open the educational environment to focus on innovation, results, and valuing essential skills:

> Substantial research literature indicates that positive teacher-student relationships (TSRs) promote students' academic achievement. One explanation is that students are more motivated to learn when they have positive relationships with teachers (Urdan & Schoenfelder, 2006). However, another plausible explanation is that teachers engage in higher-quality teaching practices when they

> have positive relationships with students. This is important because research on school effectiveness consistently identifies high-quality instruction as one of the largest school-based contributors to students' academic achievement (Scheerens, 2001; Thoonen et al., 2011). (Li et al., 2022)

Anecdotally, Indigo has seen that in traditional school models, students are most innovative in elementary school with a minor decline in middle school and a more distinctive decline in high school. What Indigo has heard from students and staff alike is that increased standardized tests in middle school and starting to figure out student "tracks" in high school start the decline. Additionally, in high school all students express the feeling of being over tested, and eleventh graders feel increased pressure to achieve high grades and test scores for university or college placement.

WPIs taken during the pandemic showed that teachers scores increased the most in innovation; however, the established system of tasks and compliance has the potential to reverse this trend. Administrators tend to score lower in innovation because the system's pressure can kill their creativity.

The data are clear and compelling. Pedro Noguera, dean of the Rossier School of Education at the University of Southern California, when reviewing the data stated, "Many of us talk about these issues but Kirtman has data to substantiate what we are saying" (personal communication, March 2022). As Pedro and Joaquin Noguera said in their ASCD article, "Creating Clarity on Equity in Schools," "The schools that make the greatest progress in meeting their equity goals work to create a culture that prioritizes students' needs. This means faculty and staff must be curious about students' needs and students' interests" (Noguera & Noguera, 2023).

Unfortunately, the task-oriented, compliant world of education puts pressure on educators that decreases engagement in what interests students and instead focuses on testing and curriculums designed to meet state and federal standards. Therefore, we see the students' leadership traits decreasing throughout their high school years. Their voices are often not considered and the lack of opportunities to engage in innovation and apply their education to real life has a negative effect on their performance.

The teachers become more task oriented through their years of teaching and can become less responsive to what students need to learn based on the Portrait of the Graduate. A focus only on academics and standardized tests, which do not focus on essential skills, decreases student engagement.

Efforts such as project-based learning, capstone projects, student agency, restorative practices, and other methods of engaging students in their own learning are designed to show real-world applications. We should make real-life education part of all our efforts.

ACADEMICS OR BEHAVIOR

One assistant principal in an urban education system once showed me a list of students: all the white students had recommendations for academic solutions, whereas all the students of color had recommendations for behavioral discipline. He believed the teachers did not realize that they were providing two different approaches to white students and students of color. The assistant principal showed the data to the principal and the entire faculty as if it were from a different school. The principal commented that her school would never allow that to happen. The assistant principal then divulged that it was their own school's data.

The principal, to her credit, looked at the data and worked with the faculty on high expectations for learning for all students. Goals were set to make sure all students were engaged in their learning and that discipline was a last resort, not an immediate reaction.

Dr. Pedro Galaviz, superintendent of Canutillo Independent School District in El Paso, Texas, who has achieved an A rating for the state for student achievement, has said that we must set high expectations for all students:

> Too many people have said, but what about that Latino student who has very little support at home and may be living in an economically disadvantaged home? No matter what the conditions are at home the high standards remain the same. Especially for first generation students we need to maintain high standards. They have not been negatively affected by the message that they cannot learn or need lower standards. For the teachers and the students that need extra support that is where equity comes in. Some teachers and students can meet our high standards without

a lot of help. Therefore, we can free up instructional coaches or extra support for students where the needs are the greatest. (Personal communication, January 2021)

To foster an environment of high expectations, we need all elements of the education community to work interdependently. It is important to see all support services as interdependent parts of a system focused on student achievement.

The custodian, the food service worker, the data specialist, the IT specialist, the facilities manager, and the parents all play important roles in the educational process. We must bring them in to help us set high expectations with the challenges students are facing. "Research shows that when parents feel respected and valued, they are more likely to reinforce school learning objectives with their children (Lawrence-Lightfoot, 1999; Valdés, 1996), and strains between parents and school staff are less likely" (Noguera & Noguera, 2023).

STRATEGIES FOR SETTING HIGH EXPECTATIONS

Setting high expectations for students from all backgrounds is crucial for promoting equity and excellence in education. Here are several strategies a district can implement to achieve this goal.

1. Cultivate a Culture of High Expectations
   - Leadership Commitment: Ensure that district and school leaders consistently communicate the belief that all students can achieve high levels of success.
   - Vision and Mission Statements: Include the commitment to high expectations for all students in the district's vision, mission statements, and Portrait of a Graduate.
2. Professional Development
   - Training and Coaching for Educators: Provide ongoing professional development focused on North Star and the integration of SEL and equity.
3. Curriculum and Instruction
   - Rigorous Curriculum: Ensure that the curriculum is challenging and engaging for all students, regardless of background.

- Differentiated Instruction: Implement instructional strategies that meet the diverse needs of students, allowing all to reach their full potential.

4. Data-Informed Decision-Making
   - Data Analysis: Regularly review data on student performance across different demographic groups to identify and address gaps.
   - Setting Benchmarks: Establish clear, measurable goals for student achievement, and monitor progress toward these goals.
5. Support Systems
   - Intervention Programs: Develop and implement academic support programs for students who are struggling.
   - Social-Emotional Support: Provide resources and support for students' social and emotional well-being as part of the goals and strategies of meeting the Portrait of the Graduate.
6. Family and Community Partnerships
   - Family Engagement: Engage families in their children's education through regular communication and involvement opportunities. Be explicit that parents are your partners in student education.
   - Community Partnerships: Partner with community organizations to provide additional resources and support for students.
7. Recognition and Celebration
   - Celebrating Achievements: Recognize and celebrate the achievements of students from all backgrounds to reinforce high expectations.
   - Role Models: Highlight success stories and provide role models from diverse backgrounds.
8. Inclusive Practices
   - Diverse Representation: Ensure that teaching materials and school activities reflect the diversity of the student population.
   - Student Voice: Include student perspectives in decision-making processes, ensuring that their needs and aspirations are considered.
9. Intrinsic Accountability
   - Evaluate Progress: Regularly review the effectiveness of strategies, and adjust as needed.
   - Transparent Reporting: Communicate progress and challenges transparently to stakeholders, including students, families, and the community.

John Pierce, former high school principal and leadership coach, related an example of high expectations for students and faculty in the following vignette.

RAISING EXPECTATIONS

In the early stages of implementing the Massachusetts Comprehensive Assessment System (MCAS) our high school projected the incoming freshman class to include sixty students who were underachieving in all subjects. There was strong consensus that we needed to develop a systemic strategy that would effectively promote high achievement for students who were likely to fail.

We went through the following decision-making process:

1. If we continued to treat everyone the same, we would never get equal results.
2. Expectations for students must be appropriately high, positive, and matched with enormous encouragement and support.
3. All teaching must utilize differentiated instruction, including flexible class groupings.
4. Class size must be capped at ten to twelve students to meet the starting points for every learner.

We took the following strategic actions:

- We created five new sections for English, math, social studies, and science, capping each at twelve students. This was funded by increasing the class sizes in the accelerated and AP classes. Two or three more students in accelerated or AP classes would not negatively affect the students.
- The most skilled teachers in each department were recruited for these new classes.
- We also recruited junior and senior students as teacher assistants from our internship program to facilitate the differentiation of instruction and multiple groupings. As teacher assistants they would be directly involved in teaching and not simply printing materials. Their strong presence immediately affected the seriousness and behavior of underclassmen in their charge.
- The teacher assistants earned elective credit and received endorsements for future college recommendations.

- During the summer prior to implementing this strategy, the principal met with every one of the sixty students and their parents to explain this initiative. This included discussions regarding concerns about labeling and mobility into advanced classes in subsequent schedules for the next school year. They all enthusiastically agreed to participate in this initiative.

Here are the tangible results in each of the subsequent four years:

1. As sophomores, many of our original sixty students were scheduled into individual and multiple standard college prep classes. In subsequent years, many more transitioned into standard or accelerated courses. In year four, there were only a handful of students remaining in this cohort.
2. All of the original sixty students passed the mandatory statewide MCAS and met graduation requirements.
3. Our entire school community witnessed the success that can be realized with a growth mindset, differentiated instruction, flexible grouping, and safety nets for underachieving students.
4. Absenteeism, tardiness, and discipline issues for the sixty students involved were remarkably low.

As we raise our expectations for students and staff, we need to have high expectations for all constituencies. Parents are a key group that need to have high expectations for their children. However, we have no direct control over parents' behavior. The following example is how we can raise parent expectations by how we view a parent's role as a partner in the education process.

It is time to change from parent involvement and engagement to partnership. It is also time to understand that our student body has changed and that parents can bring new perspectives to educational design.

Dr. Sybil Knight Burney, former superintendent of Harrisburg, Pennsylvania, formed a parent advisory committee whose mission was to offer feedback on the district's plans. More importantly, the parents would be educated and exposed to school improvement models and actively involved in making decisions that affected the entire system. One member of the parent advisory group, Malicke Parham said,

> The parent advisory committee offered the parents an inside view into what it takes to operate a school district and provide counsel to decision makers. It was a welcoming endeavor granted by a servant leader. Dr. Knight Burney did not have to open her door to include parents; however, she understood the value that each person brought to the table and the lasting relationships it would create. Our greatest tools are time and others—and these were harnessed in a very impactful way—a lesson cherished and carried for a lifetime. With her continuous encouragement, this experience was added motivation for me to become a teacher in the district. (Knight Burney, personal communication, March 2024)

Parent engagement means that new ideas, viewpoints, and practices will be introduced. Outside experts can be valuable as consultants and coaches using their knowledge, but internal leaders need to lead the change efforts. This approach gains ownership from teachers and creates sustainable change.

BEWARE OF SYSTEMS THAT PERPETUATE LOW EXPECTATIONS

Special education is a critical department in every school district. Every student by law is required to have the accommodations they need. Although important, the special education world unfortunately can lower expectations for students. The Individualized Education Program (IEP) is the process for defining and implementing the law. Although the IEP is the core tool for special education, there can be too much focus on process, and the IEP can become the result and not the plan for the student to receive support.

Unfortunately, special education being separated from general education classes can result in teachers and principals believing that it is not their role to improve student achievement for all students. As one special education director once said to me, "When an issue emerges with a special education student, they call in the calvary (my staff) to take care of the problem."

However, there are many special education teachers who have high expectations for all their students. My sister was a special education teacher for forty years. She was results oriented and looked for any approach or tool to help her students achieve. She was an early adopter of technology because she thought it would even the playing field for her students to achieve. We need to move to a results-first approach for special education students. The Portrait of the Graduate provides direction on the combination of academic content and essential skills. The outcomes for special education students are the starting place, and the IEP is the plan to meet those goals.

There have been numerous approaches to broaden the focus from special education to student services. Although this has helped in some districts, it is time for a change of mindset. Perhaps we should eliminate special education departments and focus on results for all students. Accommodation for learning is important for all students. This unifying approach can establish ownership of teaching and learning for all students with principals, administrators, and teachers. This shift can raise the standards for special education, and all students, with the proper support in place.

Separating training and coaching for regular education and special education has contributed to the silos that exist. Dr. Laura Schwalm, a retired and highly recognized superintendent from Garden Grove, California, had one department for regular education and special education that focused on all students. She believed that this approach was effective and contributed to the success of her district.

HIGH EXPECTATIONS COME FROM WITHIN STUDENTS

As Chapter 3 outlined, high expectations for students are driven by the Portrait of the Graduate. All educators need to adopt a new paradigm that high expectations come from within the student as they learn how to take personal responsibility for their success. We must also have the same belief system for staff.

As Roman Stearns (2024) stated in his recent white paper, "A student-centered approach to education, that to scale student success and making the student the center of the learning there four shifts that must be made immediately:

1. Promote competency-based education.
2. Normalize student-centered experiential learning.
3. Center a whole-child vision.
4. Shift from measuring knowledge to assessing durable skills."

This book provides you with an approach to accomplish all four recommendations. The Portrait of a Graduate provides the vehicle to drive the plan. However, district leaders and teachers need to commit to an intrinsic, continuous improvement process to make this shift. Modeling high expectations to move toward intrinsic motivation for success is embodied in the following vignette.

CLEAN THE CAFETERIA

High expectations for student success are internally driven for leaders. Jill Krieger was a new high school assistant principal and walked into the cafeteria every day to see garbage on the floor and on the tables. During each lunch wave, students added their garbage to the piles. There were rumors that the superintendent was concerned about the lack of cleanliness and unhappy with the principal. Although this was talked about, no one was taking any action to address the problem. Krieger decided that this situation needed to change now. She was results oriented (high achievement in the WPI). She grabbed a garbage can, went around to each table, and asked the students to put their garbage in the can. The students began throwing the garbage away without question. The maintenance staff and security people told Krieger that she should not have to do this because she was an assistant principal. She said she would do this every day until the problem was resolved. Without asking them to join her, staff members also took garbage cans and joined in cleaning up the cafeteria. Some students came to Krieger and said they were sorry that she had to do this. A few even started pushing garbage cans to tables. Within a few days the garbage was no longer a problem, and the cafeteria was clean. Krieger no longer had to do this alone. She knew the students needed to do this on their own. However, to get to that result, she modeled the behavior, which resulted in everyone being responsible, including the students. What does this have to do with student achievement? If high expectations are modeled, they become a new way of life and the new normal. If the expectations are low, everyone lowers their standards. A messy cafeteria flows over to expectations for learning.

The superintendent snuck through the back door of the cafeteria a few days later and was shocked that the cafeteria was clean. The superintendent and principal did not achieve any results through their hierarchy. It was a results-oriented assistant principal who refused to lower standards who made the difference. Krieger went on to become a high school principal and superintendent and now is a leadership coach.

This vignette demonstrates that internal accountability is more powerful than an external hierarchy to obtain sustainable results. Titles and hierarchy are often too rigid in education. If results for students are a clear North Star, titles are of less concern. Krieger had a sense of urgency for results and did not ask for permission to move forward. Unfortunately, most titles below the senior leaders are about only support and tasks. There are too many titles such as coordinators, support staff, secretary, assistant principal, accountability officer, and parent coordinator. We need to change titles to reflect more focus on leadership for results, such as associate principal, deputy directors, office managers, director of parent partnerships, to empower people to act and not wait for the people above to solve problems. Intrinsic accountability (see Chapter 6) will allow leaders to make the shift on assessing staff performance to be coherent with the shift for students. The shift is to have student and staff agency. If people are responsible for their own actions and need to use results to drive their work, then titles do not matter as much. People can provide feedback to colleagues who they can value as supportive to their success. The top-down evaluation is not as powerful as people owning their own development and helping their colleagues succeed.

CHANGE THE PARADIGM ON SETTING HIGH EXPECTATIONS FOR STAFF

Begin with the mindset that if you treat all staff with respect and provide deep coaching, they will succeed and learn. Changing the paradigm on setting high expectations for staff starts at the cabinet level in a district. The superintendent and the senior team need to commit to coaching to develop the leadership capacity of all staff. The tone of coaching should be more motivational than top-down accountability (see Chapter 6). The following is a framework for how a superintendent can coach senior leaders who then can be a model of coaching for their staff.

A FRAMEWORK FOR COACHING

1. Establish a framework for deeper discussion or coaching with each coach. Set a high-expectations mindset.
    - Be clear on the outcomes.
    - Present data without judgment.
    - Use the WPI or any leadership self-assessment throughout the framework.

(Continued)

(Continued)

2. Practice integrative thinking.
   - Be direct and genuine on performance issues with all people, including people of color.
   - Never lower expectations, but coach for results.
   - Establish a sense of urgency for results, but promote introspection about one's own style of leadership.
   - Be direct on performance issues with people of color. One can be sensitive to cultural and life issues and still be direct. This will require being able to discuss the cultural and life issues as an open and explicit part of the conversation.
3. Understand and be explicit about what your North Star looks like for student and staff performance. The North Star sets a clear direction; however, defining your goals at high levels is critical. One district superintendent in California said she defined results through growth. However, when presented with the viewpoint that excellence is the outcome and growth is the process with benchmarks along the way, the superintendent changed her definition to excellence.
4. Change from an accountability to a coaching culture. A coaching culture is how employees can control their own narrative to success. The role of all administrators is to model behaviors and coach people to success. This will be further explained in Chapter 6.
5. Discuss and put in norms for each constituency on how they can operate and lead from a high expectations mindset. For example, meetings can start with an assumption of positive intent, not with blame or accusations when a result is not achieved.
6. Shift the language we use to scholars instead of students, and provide development for all professional, including classified.

   students > scholars

   staff > professionals

   at risk > at promise

   As stated earlier, Dr. Victor Rios—who obtained his doctorate from University of California, Berkeley—has built his career on changing how we talk about at-risk kids to at-promise kids, which is having a positive impact on education nationally.

7. Stop the Dance of the Lemons practice. This is when a poor performer is moved to another school or a different role just to get them out. Everyone must commit to continuous learning. Through the fit process outlined in Chapter 4, each leader can make sure the fit works for the employee and the organization. If the employee does not fit the organization or the organization does not fit them, moving them to another role will not result in success. A poor performer in a new setting with an intrinsic motivation to succeed will still be a lemon in the new setting.

8. Recruit talented people by using interview questions and reference checking to look for candidates who have high expectations and a good a track record. As stated in Chapter 3, recruitment can start with referrals from talented staff.

9. Remove the words "failure" and "I am not perfect" from your language. Failure for one may be success for others. The goal is always continuous improvement to desired results. "I am not perfect" implies that perfection is the outcome. This put the emphasis on the person and their image, not the results for the students. The goal is never perfection if we believe in continuous improvement.

10. Learn how to give direct feedback that is results oriented to raise expectations. Break the cycle of people talking about others behind their back. One can be direct and supportive at the same time as an integrative leader.

11. Move away from SMART or SMARTIE goals to goals with indicators of success. Although SMART and SMARTIE goals are popular in education, the process tends to lower expectations. The word *realistic* tends to result in staff setting goals that they know they can reach. The fear of evaluation and failure can send a subtle message to staff to set low goals and expectations. If we move to indictors of success, we are not trying to lower standards to make sure we get a positive evaluation. If people do not meet an indicator, they are not failures. If an indicator a 30% improvement in math scores is set and not met, we examine why without blame. This allows staff to learn, improve, and not fear failure.

CHAPTER SUMMARY

Every district will say they have high expectations for all students and staff. However, this is easy to say but exceedingly difficult to implement. As this chapter has shown, students have relatively high expectations for success. However, our system of tasks and compliance tends to put pressure on teachers, and they become distracted from setting high expectations for students and maintaining that focus. The North Star sets the definition of success for students, and the staff needs to never lower the desire for student excellence. This chapter outlines how you can stay the course of excellence and not get distracted by new initiatives, behavioral challenges, or rules and regulations. Every educator has a story about a student or staff member who went well beyond their expectations. We owe it to every student and educator to create a culture of excellence that expects and supports people to achieve at their highest level.

CHAPTER TAKEAWAYS

- Look at all the standards of excellence for students and staff, and keep them high.
- Consider rethinking special education as separate from other student and staff expectations.
- Fully utilize all current and outside resources to support excellence (parents, community, partnerships, etc.).
- Restructure and assign all district-level administrators as results oriented support partners for every school in the district. District leaders should be visible in schools. Create data charts that delineate the academic progress of all students, and clearly pinpoint the challenge areas that must be prioritized and addressed. As important as academic data are, have a deep understanding of students and their motivators and preferred work styles.
- If you set high expectations for all staff, most will rise to the occasion. The ones who don't do not fit your organization. They can be coached out.
- Remembering language is important to monitor to create a culture of high expectations. Words like *blame, failure,* and *at-risk* lower expectations.

- Move to a self-directed student and staff agency mindset.
- Parents are the child's first teachers; set high expectations for their partnership, but meet them where they are.
- Continually connect to all constituencies inside the district and in the community about the high expectations culture and how they can contribute.

QUESTIONS FOR REFLECTION

1. Do you believe you set high standards? If so, how do you maintain them during difficult times?
2. How can you begin examining when and why you or others lower standards for students or staff?
3. What are some examples of when you set and stayed with high standards. What was the result?
4. What are examples when standards were compromised? What was the result?

6

INTRINSIC ACCOUNTABILITY

Student and Staff Agency

Learning Intentions

1. Clarify why the accountability system is out of alignment with the North Stars of districts.
2. Clarify why intrinsic accountability is critical to pivoting leadership.
3. Learn how to implement a more effective and sustainable means of assessing and motivating performance.
4. Understand how intrinsic accountability is the lynchpin for attracting and retaining the workforce needed to ensure student success.

We have explored why education is at a crossroads. The current strategies in education are resulting in a lack of student achievement, a decrease in student and staff attendance, educators leaving the profession, stress reaching toxic levels for most staff, and increased gaps in student learning. This book proposes a pivot of leadership to focus on a defining a new North Star, shifting from tasks and compliance to a results culture, finding and supporting talent, building teacher leadership, and setting high expectations. The final piece of this puzzle is to examine the current accountability system in education, which is not coherent with our proposed new leadership pivot. We must align the evaluation process, which other sectors call performance reviews, with our overall results approach.

What Is the Problem We Are Trying to Solve?

Education has become obsessed with accountability. Although there is nothing wrong with the word *accountability*, it has become synonymous with a top-down process of using evaluation to make sure that educators are doing what they are supposed to do. Teachers see the accountability system in education as a process to tell them to do what they're told and be compliant.

Our research shows that compliance often works against results. When leadership watches over administrators, teachers, and staff to make sure they are compliant, they tend to feel constrained and lose their focus on the North Star. The outcome of overcompliance is that staff fear that creativity and innovation will get them in trouble. The current accountability system is deficit driven, not opportunity or success driven.

> More than a decade ago, policymakers made a multi-billion-dollar bet that strengthening teacher evaluation would lead to better teaching, which in turn would boost student achievement. But new research shows that, overall, those efforts failed: Nationally, teacher evaluation reforms over the past decade had no impact on student test scores or educational attainment. (Will, 2021)

The accountability system in education has not created sustainable improvement for student success. High-stakes testing has put more compliance pressure on the system, which has not produced any significant improvement.

Accountability has resulted in an evaluation system that is seen by most educators as punitive. Educational leaders often say they need to hold people accountable through the evaluation process. This is an external concept that can be viewed by educators as that we cannot trust them to care about or be accountable for student success.

Teachers fear what seems like a "gotcha" environment and can become compliant, which has been shown to have a negative effect on student learning. We tend to treat educators as if they are not professionals and cannot be trusted. We use data that continually show teachers are failing with the hope that the pressure to change will result in improvements.

John Pierce (personal communication, 2024), a former high school principal and leadership coach, has said that we need to establish and support a definition for professionals. He has recommended that administrators discuss what it means to be a professional, establish norms for behavior, and then hold themselves and their colleagues accountable to these behaviors. These norms will demonstrate respect for the entire team as professionals.

WHAT IS A PROFESSIONAL?

1. We know, understand, and can do what others without our training and experience cannot.
2. We consistently develop our capacity to advance our professional effectiveness.
3. We self-regulate and never have to be told to do what we know, or should know, is professionally proper.
4. We place social pressure on and provide feedback to those who do not conduct themselves professionally.

Blaming culture in education is driving people away from the sector. Edmond Deming, the founder of organizational development in the business world, understood this problem. The Deming 94-6 Rule suggests that 94% of problems within an organization are caused by the system, whereas only 6% are attributable to individual employees. Thus, it is the system, not the individual, that causes the problems. Therefore, an accountability system that is perceived as blaming individuals and is focused on externally driven data (which has been seen as punitive by most teachers) will not produce better results. "Daniel Pink (2009) has shown conclusively that this carrot-and-stick approach works at best for only the most mechanical tasks, not for anything that requires ingenuity or commitment. You don't get coherence by imposing diktats" (Fullan & Quinn 2015).

The following is a quote from the business world about evaluation processes being conducted only once a year that has relevance to education:

> Regular conversations about performance and development change the focus to building the workforce your organization needs to be competitive both today and years from now. Business researcher Josh Bersin estimates that about 70% of multinational companies are moving toward this model, even if they haven't arrived quite yet. (Cappelli & Tavis, 2016)

Many districts realize that there is no data or research that shows that evaluation improves performance (Kirtman, 2014). The evaluation process is after the fact and has little effect on sustainable improvement. In fact, virtually no educational leaders or teachers nationally seem to believe that evaluation improves performance. Yet we stay the course.

We must decide on whether it is time to hire talent and trust them to educate our children. This trust is not blind because it needs to be coupled with an intrinsic ownership of results for students. If we are having continual "fit" conversations, as outlined in Chapter 4, we will surround the students with models and practices that motivate them to build the skills, competencies, and knowledge to be successful. State and federal government and many leaders fear giving up control to the students and staff when, ironically, we do not have control now.

As we have shown throughout this book, student agency and teacher leadership are keys to pivoting leadership in finding and developing talent and increasing student success. The process of how we outline improvement is self-directed based on a clear North Star with coaching and continuous feedback. Having an externally driven evaluation system that is not self-directed creates tension within the education process. "Almost fifteen years ago, Richard Elmore (2004) said that no amount of external accountability will be successful in the absence of internal accountability. He added that internal accountability logically precedes external accountability" (Fullan & Kirtman 2019). We must build our internal, intrinsically based system of accountability to increase our external results. We need to be coherent with the same philosophy for student and staff success. Move toward the intrinsic, continuous improvement model we are proposing, and you will see the changes and success you always hoped would occur for yourself and the students.

Pivoting from external accountability and evaluation to internally driven continuous improvement is the final piece of our new approach to success. A key principle from Kirtman's research and experience and Fullan's international viewpoint is the role of accountability. "Intrinsic accountability creates a culture of continuous improvement. Creativity, risk taking, and innovation thrive in a culture of intrinsic accountability" (Fullan & Kirtman 2019). Innovation is paramount in the education and preparation of students for today's constantly changing world.

There is significant data that continuous feedback improves performance rather top-down evaluations. Applying integrated thinking, you can legally meet the needs of evaluation and set up a process where employees can have control over their own narrative to success. With a culture of high expectations and a clear North Star, all employees can move to a continuously improving culture with increased student success.

This culture isn't for everyone. Some people want to be told what to do and do their job for a paycheck. To establish an intrinsically driven continuous improvement culture, you need to hire people who are internally motivated. Therefore, the hiring process needs to find people who want to control their own narrative and are committed to student results. This attitude and mindset are critical in the recruitment and hiring of people.

Our current process of progressive discipline and improvement plans are not aligned with an intrinsically motivated results culture. A performance improvement plan (PiP) is a documentation and firing process, not an improvement process. It is externally driven and tends to be ineffective. "PiPs don't improve performance. They may even do more harm than good" (Glazer, 2018). Often the requirements of a PiP are so basic that a person can meet its components and not improve performance. In addition, when someone is taken off a PiP, the performance tends to decrease again. Some people on a PiP, even if they do improve, feel upset and humiliated from being put on a plan in the first place. However, a coaching process can avoid this issue and work much better with clear outcomes for students as the driving force. Effective coaching driven from the Portrait of the Graduate goals, with a trust but verify approach, will increase the results for staff. If the process is driven by a person who coaches and holds accountability for results tied to student performance, rather than focusing on completion of tasks, the results will be sustainable and long-lasting.

The fear of an intrinsically driven continuous improvement process can be that it may not work. If a supervisor is coaching and uses data tied to the Portrait of the Graduate, the chance of improvement is much higher. Combined with fit conversations, the process will determine if the job is a fit for the person and the district. If a person does not improve, as outlined earlier, they can be coached out of the district. Unfortunately, districts rely on an accountability system and PiPs to remove people from their jobs for poor performance. It may seem easier to put someone on a PiP and abandon coaching too early. In this way we drive people out of districts in a market where it is hard to find talent.

The process of developing and monitoring PiPs takes a lot of for the principal and for the teacher. Because there is little chance of success, these extrinsic processes need to shift to being intrinsic and driven by the staff, which will free up countless hours. This time can be used to coach people to success, communicate with parents, and determine ways to increase student achievement.

One can ask the question that if a person does not achieve results and does not respond to coaching, how will the person be held accountable? The answer is that the employee is accountable through student results. If they are not responding to coaching, the supervisor documents their behavior. The supervisor then tells the employee the results need to be improved and that the employee has a choice to engage in the process to improve or to not change. If the employee does not choose to change, they must be reminded that they made a choice to not focus on student results, which is paramount. Then the formal documentation process will result in them being removed from their position. This result is their choice; no one did this to them.

The following is a vignette that shows how this process works in real life.

TALENTED BUT DISCONNECTED FROM STUDENTS

Ms. X was a talented content and instructional teacher who had high expectations of her students. However, she did not connect well to how the students were performing. She would not slow down to make sure every student was learning. The principal wanted to send her to pace training and told her to slow down. The teacher took his feedback as lowering standards and expectations for learning. The principal could have put the teacher on a PiP, which could lead to Ms. X being fired or removing students in need from her classes. Either of these outcomes would have taken away the best teacher from the students in greatest need.

Instead, the principal was advised to coach Ms. X to success and recognize her for her excellent instructional skills and high expectations. The principal was coached to work collaboratively with Ms. X on how to help the students who were not learning. She needed to know that student learning was the expectation. She would no longer be able to fail students and maintain that she was not the problem if students weren't learning.

Coaching began by communicating to Ms. X that her talents and high expectations could be used to connect to all the students. The principal worked with her on how to maintain her high expectations and still connect and bring students to an intrinsically driven desire for success. He stated that it was important for her to affect all students, not only those she believed were committed to excellence.

The teacher said she would think about the principal's approach. Her reluctance showed that this conversation should have occurred much earlier or even when she was hired. Going forward, the principal needed to set high expectations and communicate to all staff and students that learning was the expected outcome, not only good teaching.

Although this approach takes time, when it becomes a routine part of a principal's work, the school will attract and retain talent. Letting go of a talented teacher in today's teacher crisis is a poor short- and long-term strategy:

> When human capital was plentiful, the focus was on which people to let go, which to keep, and which to reward—and for those purposes, traditional appraisals (with their emphasis on individual accountability) worked pretty well. But when talent was in shorter supply, as it is now, developing people became a greater concern—and organizations had to find new ways of meeting that need. (Cappelli & Tavis, 2016)

Kate Dias (personal communication, 2024), Connecticut Education Association union president, has told superintendents that excellent teachers are as upset with poor teachers as administrators. There is common ground with unions on the shift to intrinsic accountability. Most union leaders agree that if the results are clear and the expectations are reasonable, then teachers will focus on student achievement. If a teacher is motivated and treated as a professional, and has a voice that is respected, they will not hide from results.

It is also important to define when evaluations need to be more top-down. If there is a need for more severe action on performance based on an egregious situation, a top-down approach may help protect students.

TEACHER AND PRINCIPAL PARTNERSHIPS IN SCHOOL LEADERSHIP

A principal in a rural district felt alone and not supported by district leadership. She was thinking of leaving to find a better fit for her goals. Her coach proposed a new approach for the principal to pivot for her growth and the success of her students.

This rural school had no assistant principal, but it did have strong union leadership. The coach encouraged the principal to form a leadership team—a true leadership team of teachers including union leadership. Although an excellent principal, her high expectations for staff and students sometimes caused grievances from the union, which had resulted in an adversarial relationship.

The coach suggested a shared leadership model. Although the principal would maintain the final decision-making authority, the team would work collaboratively to share leadership, and their voices would be valued. The new norm for this team was that the principal would not say that she had make decisions on her own unless it was an extreme situation or a personnel or manner that required privacy. The union agreed not to automatically file grievances in the face of complaints; instead, the union would bring the issue to the leadership team meeting and discuss a solution that met the needs of the students and respected the teacher.

All the teachers on the leadership team agreed to start on this journey of creative problem-solving rather than top-down accountability. The principal decided to stay and signed her contract for one year to try out this new approach. The teachers were excited that they were valued and that everyone wanted students to succeed.

The goal is to move the accountability and evaluation process to a self-directed, continuous improvement process that motivates people and decreases fear.

STEPS FOR MOVING TO A SELF-DIRECTED, CONTINUOUS IMPROVEMENT PROCESS

Step 1: All constituents need to understand their role in the implementation of intrinsic accountability. Internal accountability occurs when individuals and groups willingly take on personal, professional, and collective responsibility for continuous improvement and success for all students (Fullan & Quinn 2015).

Step 2: All evaluation documents and tools need to adjust the language to internally driven practices.

Step 3: Self-assessments need to drive the intrinsic accountability process (see Appendix A). This can include leadership assessments (i.e., the WPI or DiSC and Values) and a self-rating tool on behaviors aligned to the North Star. Each employee or team should choose a leadership competency for continuous improvement (i.e., Kirtman's Seven Competencies; see Appendix F).

Step 4: Metrics and indicators of success need to be clear for staff to self-assess their work in relation to student success.

Step 5: All administrators need to see themselves as coaches rather than evaluators with benchmarks for success built into all conversations with individuals and teams.

Step 6: External metrics such as state standardized tests must be incorporated into the self-assessment process. "By investing in focused capacity building, leaders are developing internal accountability in which the group is accountable for its performance, and these leaders interface willingly and openly to the external state accountability system" (Kirtman & Fullan 2017).

Step 7: Create a culture of coaching to results. Train and coach people on how to coach to bring out successful practices from staff.

Step 8: Create a culture that openly shares success stories that are not seen as competitive or self-aggrandizing.

By using the existing evaluation process, addressing state standards, and adding time for self-evaluation and reflection into the process of evaluating, teachers and staff become more effective and supervisors receives more buy-in from those being evaluated. Christina Smith (personal communication, 2024), principal of Gateway Community Charters, adjusted the current process in her district to move toward the intrinsic evaluation process by adding in the following three steps (in italics):

- Educator completes self-evaluation. (August)
- *Educators create goals. (September)*
- *Manager completes formal observation(s) and debrief(s). (September-April)*
- *Manager completes informal observations and provides immediate feedback. (September-April)*
- Educator reflects on progress of goals. (January)
- Educator reflects on growth (self-evaluation) and goals. (April-May)
- Manager reviews evaluation with educator. (April-May)

She updated the Gateway Charters rating language to the Association of California School Administrators (ACSA) rating language, which is more motivating, growth-oriented, and aligned with an intrinsic accountability mindset. These changes in the rating areas are more collaborative and empowering for internal development. Terms like *exploring* or *innovating* replace terms such as *proficiency* and *below standards*. She also asked questions that involved reflection rather than judgment. This process created a dialogue on continuous improvement.

Now Smith is working on increasing the data side of teacher development. Because the district has a Portrait of a Graduate, data on student achievement and measurements for the essential skills will be built into the discussions between her and each teacher. In addition, the teacher will complete the Workplace Personality Inventory (WPI) and add other leadership assessments into the conversation to improve their skills and behaviors. This will allow the teacher to reflect on how they can adjust to improve student success.

In a pilot Smith completed last year, teachers were positive about the adjusted evaluation process. They noted that they felt less judged and more empowered to improve their practice. Teachers also reflected that if a district were using this new intrinsically driven process, that would motivate them to seek employment there.

Figure 6.1 shows a revised evaluation tool using the WPI and the Seven Competencies as part of the goal setting for continuous improvement for administrators throughout the district. "It is important to realize that no one is perfect and at the highest level on all of the seven competencies; the best leaders strive to improve on each one" (Kirtman & Fullan, 2017). You can begin your own improvement process by using the Self-Reflection on the Seven Competencies (see Appendix A). In addition, to get a more meaningful and complete look at your leadership, have a peer assess you on the Seven Competencies (Appendix B). Using both sets of data can focus your improvement process. In Appendix D you will find a Leadership Development Plan that can be used in conjunction with the self-assessment. These tools are a great starting point to pivot your leadership and reduce your stress.

6.1 A Sample ACSA Self-Evaluation Based on State Standards in California

Self-Assessment & Reflection
California Standards for the Teaching Profession

Teacher Name: *Date:*

STANDARD 1: ENGAGING AND SUPPORTING ALL STUDENTS IN LEARNING

*Be sure to refer to the *Continuum of Teaching Practice* when completing this assessment.			Emerging (Needs Improvement)	Exploring (Developing)	Applying/Integrating (Meets Standard)		Innovating (Exceeds Standard)
1.1	Using knowledge of students to engage them in learning	Initial					
		Final					
1.2	Connecting learning to students' prior knowledge, backgrounds, life experiences, and interests	Initial					
		Final					
1.3	Connecting subject matter to meaningful, real-life contexts	Initial					
		Final					
1.4	Using a variety of instructional strategies, resources, and technologies to meet students' diverse learning needs	Initial					
		Final					
1.5	Promoting critical thinking through inquiry, problem-solving, and reflection	Initial					
		Final					
1.6	Monitoring student learning and adjusting instruction while teaching	Initial					
		Final					

Initial Reflection

Strengths:

-

Areas of Growth:

-

Final Reflection

Strengths:

-

Areas of Growth:

-

STANDARD 2: CREATING AND MAINTAINING EFFECTIVE ENVIRONMENTS FOR STUDENT LEARNING							
*Be sure to refer to the *Continuum of Teaching Practice* when completing this assessment.			**Emerging** (Needs Improvement)	**Exploring** (Developing)	**Applying/Integrating** (Meets Standard)		**Innovating** (Exceeds Standard)
2.1	Promoting social development and responsibility within a caring community where each student is treated fairly and respectfully	Initial					
		Final					
2.2	Creating physical or virtual learning environments that promote student learning, reflect diversity, and encourage constructive and productive interactions among students	Initial					
		Final					
2.3	Establishing and maintaining learning environments that are physically, intellectually, and emotionally safe	Initial					
		Final					
2.4	*Creating a rigorous learning environment with high expectations* and appropriate support for all students	Initial					
		Final					
2.5	Developing, communicating, and maintaining high standards for individual and group behavior	Initial					
		Final					
2.6	Employing classroom routines, procedures, norms, and supports for positive behavior to ensure a climate in which all students can learn	Initial					
		Final					
2.7	Using instructional time to optimize learning	Initial					
		Final					

Initial Reflection

Strengths:

-

Areas of Growth:

-

Final Reflection

Strengths:

-

Areas of Growth:

-

(Continued)

(Continued)

STANDARD 3: UNDERSTANDING AND ORGANIZING SUBJECT MATTER FOR STUDENT LEARNING							
*Be sure to refer to the *Continuum of Teaching Practice* when completing this assessment.			**Emerging** (Needs Improvement)	**Exploring** (Developing)	**Applying/Integrating** (Meets Standard)		**Innovating** (Exceeds Standard)
3.1	Demonstrating knowledge of subject matter academic content standards	Initial					
		Final					
3.2	Applying knowledge of student development and proficiencies to ensure student understanding of subject matter	Initial					
		Final					
3.3	Organizing curriculum to facilitate student understanding of the subject matter	Initial					
		Final					
3.4	Utilizing instructional strategies that are appropriate to the subject matter	Initial					
		Final					
3.5	Using and adapting resources, technologies, and standards-aligned instructional materials, including adopted materials, to make subject matter accessible to all students	Initial					
		Final					
3.6	Addressing the needs of English learners and students with special needs to provide equitable access to the content	Initial					
		Final					

Initial Reflection

Strengths:

•

Areas of Growth:

•

Final Reflection

Strengths:

•

Areas of Growth:

•

STANDARD 4: PLANNING INSTRUCTION AND DESIGNING LEARNING EXPERIENCES FOR ALL STUDENTS

*Be sure to refer to the *Continuum of Teaching Practice* when completing this assessment.			Emerging (Needs Improvement)	Exploring (Developing)	Applying/Integrating *(Meets Standard)*		Innovating (Exceeds Standard)
4.1	Using knowledge of students' academic readiness, language proficiency, cultural background, and individual development to plan instruction	Initial					
		Final					
4.2	Establishing and articulating goals for student learning	Initial					
		Final					
4.3	Developing and sequencing long- and short-term instructional plans to support student learning	Initial					
		Final					
4.4	Planning instruction that incorporates appropriate strategies to meet the learning needs of all students	Initial					
		Final					
4.5	Adapting instructional plans and curricular materials to meet the assessed learning needs of all students	Initial					
		Final					

Initial Reflection

Strengths:

•

Areas of Growth:

•

Final Reflection

Strengths:

•

Areas of Growth:

•

(Continued)

(Continued)

STANDARD 5: PLANNING INSTRUCTION AND DESIGNING LEARNING EXPERIENCES FOR ALL STUDENTS							
*Be sure to refer to the *Continuum of Teaching Practice* when completing this assessment.			Emerging (Needs Improvement)	Exploring (Developing)	Applying/Integrating (Meets Standard)		Innovating (Exceeds Standard)
5.1	Applying knowledge of the purposes, characteristics, and uses of different types of assessments	Initial					
		Final					
5.2	Collecting and analyzing assessment data from a variety of sources to inform instruction	Initial					
		Final					
5.3	Reviewing data, both individually and with colleagues, to monitor student learning	Initial					
		Final					
5.4	Using assessment data to establish learning goals and to plan, differentiate, and modify instruction	Initial					
		Final					
5.5	Involving all students in self-assessment, goal setting, and monitoring progress	Initial					
		Final					
5.6	Using available technologies to assist in assessment, analysis, and communication of student learning	Initial					
		Final					
5.7	Using assessment information to share timely and comprehensible feedback with students and their families	Initial					
		Final					

Initial Reflection

Strengths:

•

Areas of Growth:

•

Final Reflection

Strengths:

•

Areas of Growth:

•

STANDARD 6: DEVELOPING AS A PROFESSIONAL EDUCATOR							
*Be sure to refer to the *Continuum of Teaching Practice* when completing this assessment.			**Emerging** (Needs Improvement)	**Exploring** (Developing)	**Applying/Integrating** (Meets Standard)		**Innovating** (Exceeds Standard)
6.1	Reflecting on teaching practice in support of student learning	Initial					
		Final					
6.2	Establishing professional goals, and engaging in continuous and purposeful professional growth and development	Initial					
		Final					
6.3	Collaborating with colleagues and the broader professional community to support teacher and student learning	Initial					
		Final					
6.4	Working with families to support student learning	Initial					
		Final					
6.5	Engaging local communities in the support of the instructional program	Initial					
		Final					
6.6	Managing professional responsibilities to maintain motivation and commitment to all students	Initial					
		Final					
6.7	Demonstrating professional responsibility, integrity, and ethical conduct	Initial					
		Final					

Initial Reflection

Strengths:

-

Areas of Growth:

-

Final Reflection

Strengths:

-

Areas of Growth:

-

Source: Adaptation of the CPSEL Self-Assessment by Christina Smith

CHAPTER SUMMARY

It is imperative to change the focus of your evaluation process from externally driven to intrinsically driven for sustainable change and improvement to occur. If we want strong leaders and staff to be results oriented, innovative, and motivated to improve their and their students' lives, we must have a coaching approach. The current approaches in education to evaluate performance are too top-down, using state and district rubrics to evaluate staff and especially teachers. If we want students to be self-directed learners, we must be coherent and have an intrinsically self-directed approach for staff. This chapter outlines how to pivot your leadership to a new model that focuses on results for students, not only behavior that administrators want to see from staff.

If you try to employ our other aspects of pivoting your leadership, which include the North Star, talent management and teacher leadership, and high expectations, without shifting the evaluation process, your results will be limited. Even the best districts that implement traditional, externally driven evaluation processes will have limited success.

Administrators and especially teachers need to feel they have some control over their own narrative, that is, that they are professionals and trusted to dedicate themselves to improving the success opportunities for students. If teachers do not want or are not able to focus on students, the leaderships respects their choice to leave the district. Administrators and teachers will always coach and support staff who are dedicated to continuous learning. In addition, the district and school leaders will need to model the same philosophy for leadership development and student learning.

CHAPTER TAKEAWAYS

- Change focus to continuous improvement and drive evaluation from results, not tasks.
- Move away from critical conversations to regular conversations on performance for all staff.
- Pivoting to intrinsic accountability will unlock the potential of all staff.
- Coaching to high performance is more effective than traditional evaluation processes.
- Students will perform better if their teachers are motivated to learn and improve. Teachers who enjoy their work and are less stressed have a direct and positive effect on student achievement.

- Teacher and administrative collaboration and learning will increase in a continuous improvement culture. Traditional evaluation processes tend to produce internal competition and silos.
- Intrinsic accountability will help staff become more results oriented, innovative, and willing to take risks to build capacity of staff and increase student success.
- Intrinsic accountability will improve the retention of talented staff.
- Change language with students and staff from accountability to motivation, from at risk to at promise, and from improvement plan to coaching for success.

QUESTIONS FOR REFLECTION

1. Do you agree that intrinsic accountability is more effective than extrinsic? What would you state are the advantages of intrinsic accountability?
2. Do you feel you can make this shift in your district? If so, how would you begin?
3. What are your fears and hesitations regarding a focus on intrinsic accountability?
4. What would help you deal with your fears, and who can assist you?

7

CALL TO ACTION

Rediscover Your North Star

I had a recent conversation with an experienced superintendent in Texas who is also coaching new superintendents for Texas Association for School Administrators. As part of reviewing his Workplace Personality Inventory (WPI) and coaching him how to use the results in coaching other superintendents, we had a good conversation about WPI data on leadership, my research, and its recommendations. He is an excellent superintendent dedicated to his district and students and contributes by helping other leaders succeed. However, when I reviewed his WPI, his results did not match the leader I was talking to about his goals, beliefs, and leadership principles. I explained that the WPI was about his behavior, not who he is or his ability to lead.

He responded that the WPI was, unfortunately, accurate; although he had been confident in his leadership, he felt he was losing his confidence about his judgement and decisions. He had always led by what was best for his students and was confident in his North Star, but the last few years did not show the results he wanted and expected for his district. He was starting to second guess himself. His scores were low on rule following, and he was committed to developing the capacity of leaders and to building strong teams in his district. He did not take directions from the state department of education (DOE) on compliance or other initiatives that were not tied to his North Star. However, now he was wondering if he should have been listening to the state. He said he appreciated my work but asked why he should listen to me.

I think this superintendent's reactions sum up how many leaders feel today. I previously struggled with why superintendents were following what they must know would not work in their districts. There are too many voices out there telling these fine, dedicated leaders what to do. So many leaders have truly lost their North Star.

This may explain why we are struggling in education and why so many people are leaving the profession. I responded to the Texas superintendent with empathy for how he must feel, going from strong and confident to now lacking the clarity in how to move ahead. It also made me more introspective about how I am missing the connection to these leaders and their struggle to move ahead. I said that this may be a wake-up call for us and that he needs to look within himself to determine what he believes is his North Star. This will bring back his confidence to listen and integrate viewpoints that make sense to him while staying true in the face of demands, mandates, and criticism that do not define him.

I look forward to meeting him again and coaching him to gain his new foundation and share how his story helped me learn about mine. I hope this book is a viewpoint for all leaders to consider and determine how their day-to-day work and priorities fits into their North Star. I remain confident that the concepts and data in this book will enable leaders to pivot in relation to today's and tomorrow's challenges. However, I do respect any reader's decision to incorporate other voices they may feel have more connection to their North Star as they embark on their reinvigoration as a leader.

I also mentioned to this superintendent that I have observed how the pandemic affected so many confident leaders. Suddenly, many accomplished leaders who always knew the answers and were great problem-solvers were not able to control their world. That time set everyone back several steps. Although we are still trying to move on, we need to stop and reflect on the toll the pandemic had on all of us. We suddenly did not know what to do and could not rely on the experts to give us answers. Leaders continually need to pivot their strategies to adjust to a world we can't always understand.

After reading this book, begin your self-assessment and introspective process. I recommend taking one or two leadership assessments and hiring a coach to help you shift your approach. Getting a coach is not a weakness; it is a strength. Most highly successful leaders, athletes, and artists have a coach, and some have more than one. It is hard to be reflective and honest with ourselves without assistance.

Once you have taken a deeper look at yourself, review the Four Pivots and determine if they fit your North Star. Could they help solve the problems you see in your district, such as these:

- Student achievement not improving at the level you want
- Having trouble filling key positions in district, such as teachers
- Staff are feeling overwhelmed and stressed
- Losing staff to other districts or leaving education completely for other opportunities
- Student and staff absenteeism at unacceptable levels

If these are indicative of the issues in your district, the shift proposed in this book can systemically meet your challenges and allow you the time and talent to focus on what matters. This book purposely does not provide any new initiatives, groundbreaking ideas, or exciting innovations. Instead, this book simplifies and focuses on the Four Pivots to help you navigate the world of education today. No one prepared educators for these challenges in their universities, certification processes, training programs, or even coaching. The pandemic shocked leaders who were completely unprepared but trying to adjust without guardrails or experts to guide them. These Four Pivots can provide focus, simplification, and guardrails for each leader to succeed. Each area is based on experience working with 500 school districts over thirty years, extensive research on education leaders who have succeeded, and experience from the private sector, government, and nonprofits. Because they are interconnected, it is recommended that you adopt all Four Pivots. In fact, the concept of integrated thinking (Chapter 2) explains why thinking systemically will be much more effective than grabbing onto individual approaches mired in disconnected initiatives.

Pivot 1—The North Star: Determine what your North Star is, and make sure all constituents understand how they can align their work in this clear direction.

Pivot 2—The Movement to Talent Management: Review your human resource practices, and practice talent management. Remember that process is important, but finding and retaining talent is the key to your success.

(Continued)

(Continued)

Pivot 3—High Expectations: Review your practices on setting high expectations for all students and staff. Be honest, and do not move around poor performers to other positions. Make sure you are not compromising standards for excellence for students based on social emotional learning and DEI or equity issues.

Pivot 4—Intrinsic Evaluation: Although you need to have an evaluation process legally to remove poor performers, turn the process upside down. Set up a coaching culture with intrinsic evaluation and continuous improvement. Make sure you do not focus on the other three leadership pivots and leave this one out. Shifting accountability is critical for sustainable change and success.

AN EXEMPLAR

The Vision of What Pivoting Can Mean to Staff and Students

A district in the Midwest is using these Four Pivots to reinvigorate their district. They have used the Portrait of the Graduate to establish a North Star that is focused on essential skills and integrates academics that are tied to standardized tests. Their instructional rounds build in essential skills with direct feedback to teachers on improvement and integration strategies. Teachers are helping other teachers with best practices.

The district has a leadership coaching program for all administrators and has coached leaders on how to have "fit" conversations regularly with staff. The district has employed everyone as recruiters to find talent and bring them to their district. They have reworked their interview process and reference checks to go beyond compliance and consistency to find out much more about the candidates. They established a teacher leader program to put teachers in the driver's seat on results for student achievement. The administrator's primary role is to be a coach rather than an evaluator.

High expectations are a theme for everything they do internally and externally. They are honest with each other when giving direct, quality feedback and no longer avoid conflict. Their new coaching skills allow them to coach people to success or give them choice for their future employment. The same honesty occurs around keeping high expectations for all students. They are using the North Star to drive their discussions rather than the limitations they observe with students or their families. They also focus on parent partnerships, not only involvement, to acknowledge the parent as the child's first teacher. The district does not use improvement plans for staff unless an egregious problem occurs.

They focus on continuous feedback instead of evaluation to improve performance. They do not use a rating or number system from the state (DOE). They ask all staff to self-evaluate their work based on results for students and the North Star. They then rely on coaching to improve performance. If a staff member does not engage in continuous improvement, they provide a choice; choose to engage in improving your craft, or we support you looking for a position in another district.

District leadership and staff have bought into the Four Pivots on leadership. They monitor their results in student achievement, enhancing talent, maintaining high expectations, and building a culture of continuous improvement. This is a dynamic process that will be continually monitored for results, making any necessary adjustments throughout the year.

Although the approach is not rocket science, it does demand courage and discipline. Resisting the people in all the traditional places that tell you to follow their rules is key to your leadership over the next three to five years. It does not mean shutting out people who don't agree with your North Star. It means evaluating what they are saying and building it into your strategy if it meets your goals and outcomes.

The data presented in this book provide research and credibility to verify that the Four Pivots will work for students and staff. The data will hopefully expand your viewpoint that some people who seem to not fit into our current approach may have talents that you will need in your districts and schools. The Four Pivots are the combined best practices from education and other sectors in alignment with the needs of your students and staff for sustainable change and improvement. This approach will be effective no matter what happens in education and in the country in the near future.

There are too many voices in the ears of our leaders today. This book can be seen as one more voice or a way to ward off the disconnected demands and attacks that have become the new normal in education. If you are focused and grounded, no one can pull or push you off track. This does mean that you must be a lead learner and constantly evolve your approach to meet the challenges ahead, but drive the change intrinsically because it makes sense to you and the students you serve.

So, if you are tired of doubting yourself and hearing completely disconnected advice from people within your district, the DOE, the community, your professional associations, and whoever wants to show up at your meetings and complain, do the following:

1. List the problems you see, and review them with your school board, your leadership team, the parent organization, the teacher's union, the chamber of commerce, and any other key constituency.
2. Propose the reason for pivoting your leadership.
3. Explain the Four Pivots.
4. Develop a plan, addressing each pivot area, and timeline for moving forward on your North Star
5. Bring the plan to each constituency, and ask for input.
6. Explain that you want to move ahead now, and adjust the plan based on input and results.

We often believe that we can't move ahead until we hear all voices and incorporate them into a plan. As a leader in a district or a school, you are hired to lead and to listen, learn, and adjust to achieve results. Many leaders believe they must know the right answers to every problem. An effective leader needs to carry what they believe is the right direction into every meeting. However, the real right or best answer will emerge when the leader is informed by the people on their team.

Imagine if you pivot your leadership to building a culture of results with talented and motivated staff. District and school leaders can spend more time working on strategic partnerships and engaging parents and community in the education process. Leaders today spend up to 90 percent of their time fighting internal battles and need to spend at least 50 percent of their time externally and strategically with their internal and external partners. Therefore, if you decrease your time fighting internal battles and you use that extra time to balance your time to 50% internal and 50% external, you will become more effective in preventing problems rather than always solving problems.

I hope this book gives you hope and strength to lead in any role you have now and in the future. Our children and society need you to shape the future!

APPENDICES

I suggest you take some time to evaluate your Seven Competencies to gain an understanding of where you currently are as a leader. The evaluation process suggested here has been divided into five parts (Appendices A–E). Following these evaluation tools is Appendix F, where you will find the description of the research tool and the data discussed in Chapter 1.

[illegible]tencies

In Part I (Appendix A), please respond to a series of statements related to the Seven Competencies. Assess the extent to which each statement is true for you on a scale of 1–5, with 1 indicating something that you do poorly and 5 indicating something you feel you do extremely well. After you rate yourself, make some notes about areas in which you feel you could improve.

In Part II (Appendix B), to gain a slightly different perspective on your competencies, have at least one peer who knows you well complete the same inventory about your strengths and challenges. Do your peer's results match your own, or do you see areas where your self-vision and your peer's vision do not correspond? What would a lack of correspondence indicate to you?

In Part III (Appendices C, D, and E), prioritize the areas you would like to address for improvement based on your self- and peer ratings and suggestions. Include strategies you would find helpful in the improvement process, and designate the measures of success in mastering a particular competency.

APPENDIX A

PART I—SELF-REFLECTION ON THE SEVEN COMPETENCIES

Name ______________________________ Date ____________________

1. Challenges the Status Quo

Competency	Self-Rating	Suggestions for Improvement
Delegates compliance tasks to staff	1 2 3 4 5	
Maintains focus on a vision for success	1 2 3 4 5	
Prioritizes getting results over following traditions	1 2 3 4 5	
Questions or challenges current practices	1 2 3 4 5	
Takes risks to achieve results	1 2 3 4 5	

2. Builds Trust Through Clear Communication and Expectations

Competency	Self-Rating	Suggestions for Improvement
Is direct and honest about performance expectations	1 2 3 4 5	
Follows through with actions on all commitments	1 2 3 4 5	
Makes sure there is a clear understanding based on written and verbal communications	1 2 3 4 5	
Is comfortable dealing with conflict	1 2 3 4 5	

3. Creates a Commonly Owned Plan for Success

Competency	Self-Rating	Suggestions for Improvement
Creates written plans with input of stakeholders	1 2 3 4 5	
Ensures that people buy into the plan	1 2 3 4 5	
Monitors implementation of the plan	1 2 3 4 5	
Develops clear measurement for each goal in the plan	1 2 3 4 5	
Creates short- and long-term plans	1 2 3 4 5	

4. Focuses on Team Over Self

Competency	Self-Rating	Suggestions for Improvement
Hires the best people for the team	1 2 3 4 5	
Commits to the ongoing development of a high-performance leadership team	1 2 3 4 5	
Builds a team environment	1 2 3 4 5	
Seeks critical feedback	1 2 3 4 5	
Empowers staff to make decisions and get results	1 2 3 4 5	
Supports the professional development of all staff	1 2 3 4 5	

5. Has a High Sense of Urgency for Change and Sustainable Results in Improvement Achievement

Competency	Self-Rating	Suggestions for Improvement
Quickly moves initiatives ahead	1 2 3 4 5	
Is decisive	1 2 3 4 5	
Uses instructional data to support needed change	1 2 3 4 5	
Builds systemic strategies to ensure sustainability of change	1 2 3 4 5	
Sets a clear direction for the organization	1 2 3 4 5	
Effectively deals with and manage change	1 2 3 4 5	

6. Commits to Continuous Improvement for Self

Competency	Self-Rating	Suggestions for Improvement
Has a high sense of curiosity for new ways to get results	1 2 3 4 5	
Possesses a willingness to change current practices for myself and others	1 2 3 4 5	
Listens to all team members to change practices to obtain results	1 2 3 4 5	
Takes responsibility for my own actions—no excuses	1 2 3 4 5	
Has strong self-management and self-reflecting skills	1 2 3 4 5	
Deals with and manages change effectively	1 2 3 4 5	

7. Builds External Networks and Partnerships

Competency	Self-Rating	Suggestions for Improvement
Sees my role as a leader on a broad base manner outside the work environment and community walls	1 2 3 4 5	
Understands my role as being a part of a variety of external networks for change and improvement	1 2 3 4 5	
Engage people inside and outside in two-way partnerships	1 2 3 4 5	
Uses technology to expand and manage a network of resource people	1 2 3 4 5	

APPENDIX B

PART II—PEER-REFLECTION ON THE SEVEN COMPETENCIES

Name of Peer Evaluator ______________________ Date ______________

Name of Leader Being Evaluated ______________________

1. Challenges the Status Quo

Competency	Peer Rating	Suggestions for Improvement
Delegates compliance tasks to staff	1 2 3 4 5	
Maintains focus on a vision for success	1 2 3 4 5	
Prioritizes getting results over following traditions	1 2 3 4 5	
Questions or challenges current practices	1 2 3 4 5	
Takes risks to achieve results	1 2 3 4 5	

2. Builds Trust Through Clear Communication and Expectations

Competency	Peer Rating	Suggestions for Improvement
Is direct and honest about performance expectations	1 2 3 4 5	
Follows through with actions on all commitments	1 2 3 4 5	
Makes sure there is a clear understanding based on written and verbal communications	1 2 3 4 5	
Is comfortable dealing with conflict	1 2 3 4 5	

3. **Creates a Commonly Owned Plan for Success**

Competency	Peer Rating	Suggestions for Improvement
Creates written plans with input of stakeholders	1 2 3 4 5	
Ensures that people buy into the plan	1 2 3 4 5	
Monitors implementation of the plan	1 2 3 4 5	
Develops clear measurement for each goal in the plan	1 2 3 4 5	
Creates short- and long-term plans	1 2 3 4 5	

4. **Focuses on Team Over Self**

Competency	Peer Rating	Suggestions for Improvement
Hires the best people for the team	1 2 3 4 5	
Commits to the ongoing development of a high-performance leadership team	1 2 3 4 5	
Builds a team environment	1 2 3 4 5	
Seeks critical feedback	1 2 3 4 5	
Empowers staff to make decisions and get results	1 2 3 4 5	
Supports the professional development of all staff	1 2 3 4 5	

5. Has a High Sense of Urgency for Change and Sustainable Results in Improvement Achievement

Competency	Peer Rating	Suggestions for Improvement
Quickly moves initiatives ahead	1 2 3 4 5	
Is decisive	1 2 3 4 5	
Uses instructional data to support needed change	1 2 3 4 5	
Builds systemic strategies to ensure sustainability of change	1 2 3 4 5	
Sets a clear direction for the organization	1 2 3 4 5	
Effectively deals with and manages change	1 2 3 4 5	

6. Commits to Continuous Improvement for Self

Competency	Peer Rating	Suggestions for Improvement
Has a high sense of curiosity for new ways to get results	1 2 3 4 5	
Possesses a willingness to change current practices for themselves and others	1 2 3 4 5	
Listens to all team members to change practices to obtain results	1 2 3 4 5	
Takes responsibility for their own actions—no excuses	1 2 3 4 5	
Has strong self-management and self-reflecting skills	1 2 3 4 5	
Deals with and manages change effectively	1 2 3 4 5	

7. Builds External Networks and Partnerships

Competency	Peer Rating	Suggestions for Improvement
Sees their role as a leader on a broad base manner outside the work environment and community walls	1 2 3 4 5	
Understands their role as being a part of a variety of external networks for change and improvement	1 2 3 4 5	
Engages people inside and outside in two-way partnerships	1 2 3 4 5	
Uses technology to expand and manage a network of resource people	1 2 3 4 5	

APPENDIX C

PART III—LEADERSHIP COMPETENCY AREAS FOR IMPROVEMENT SUMMARY

How Competent a Leader Are You?

Competency	Total Possible Score	Self-Rating	Peer Rating
1. Challenges the Status Quo	25		
2. Builds Trust Through Clear Communications and Expectations	20		
3. Creates a Commonly Owned Plan for Success	25		
4. Focuses on Team Over Self	30		
5. Has a High Sense of Urgency for Change and Sustainable Results in Improving Student Achievement	30		
6. Commits to Continuous Improvement for Self	30		
7. Builds External Networks and Partnerships	20		
TOTAL	180		

Prioritized Areas for Improvement/Strategies				
Competency	Self-Score	Peer Score	Strategies for Improvement	Measures for Success

APPENDIX D

LEADERSHIP DEVELOPMENT PLAN

My Workplace Personality Inventory (WPI) and DiSC Results Summary

____

____

____

____

Other Inventory Results Summary (MBTI, Colors, 360 Survey, or from lived experience)

____

____

____

____

My Strengths:

-
-
-

My Areas for Leadership Growth:

-
-
-

Potential Conflicts and Stressors:

-
-
-

Leadership and Teaming Qualities That *You* Bring to the Team:

-
-
-

School Year Goals

Based on the review of the WPI and the competency you have chosen, write goals and indicators of success.

1. Goal:

   Indicator of Success:

   Indicator of Success:

2. Goal:

   Indicator of Success:

   Indicator of Success:

3. Goal:

   Indicator of Success:

   Indicator of Success:

General Barriers to Goal Attainment:

Briefly summarize the barriers you believe could directly affect your accomplishment of your goals.

Action Plan:

Briefly outline your actions to accomplish each goal outlined above.

APPENDIX E

LEADERSHIP COMPETENCY FOCUS

After completing the self-assessments, enter your score for each of the leadership competencies. Then select one competency you'd like to focus on for this year.

Leadership Competency	Score
Challenges the Status Quo	
Builds Trust Through Clear Communications and Expectations	
Creates a Commonly Owned Plan for Success	
Focuses on Team Over Self	
Has a High Sense of Urgency for Change and Sustainable Results in Improving Student Achievement	
Commits to Continuous Improvement for Self	
Builds External Networks and Partnerships	

Choose one competency for this year's focus:

____

____

____

____

APPENDIX F

WORKPLACE PERSONALITY INVENTORY INFORMATION

The WPI was originally created by Pearson and Talent Lens Inc. to help human resource departments in the corporate world with the hiring process. It focuses on self-reported behavior at work. I have expanded the use of the WPI to inform the coaching and development of leaders and to build effective leadership teams. The results of the WPI assessment are presented using sixteen traits; each is rated using a percentile score.

These are the definitions of the sixteen leadership traits based on the research findings and the desired score ranges in the initial Pearson and Talent Lens Inc. study.

1. Achievement Orientation—Focuses on outcomes first and then backs plan to determine actions: 60 or above
2. Persistence—Stays with issues to completion and not does not let distractions derail them: 60 or above
3. Initiative—Acts on needed issues without the need to ask permission: 60 or above
4. Leadership Orientation—Is willing to be out front setting direction for the future and establishing a results culture: 60 or above
5. Social Orientation—Connects to others in your school, district, education field, and beyond for ideas and best practices: 60 and above
6. Cooperation—Connects to people and is approachable, but sometimes high scores may have trouble being direct and reality-based: less than 50
7. Concern for Others—Is caring, but high scores may let the caring block the need to put results for students first: less than 50
8. Self-Control—Controls emotions and reactions so that they can be more thoughtful in responses to situations: 50 and above
9. Stress Tolerance—Is open to critical feedback and the ability to manage stress: 50 and above
10. Flexibility and Adaptability—Adjusts to changing needs without losing focus on the outcomes: 60 and above

11. Dependability—Ensures follow through by distributing leadership to not control the work themselves: less than 50

12. Attention to Detail—Makes sure details are done well but making sure they don't get caught in the weeds to block focusing on the big picture: less than 50

13. Rule Following—Focuses on rules that are tied to outcomes but puts minimal effort into rules that are not tied to results: less than 50

14. Innovation—Is open and willing to be creative and try new approaches: 60 and above

15. Analytical Thinking—Focuses on data and the search for root causes with the ability to connect data to real stories of people: between 40 and 60

16. Independence—Doesn't wait to be told what to do or to get permission: 60 and above

In some cases, the research shows that high scores are desirable, whereas other traits with low scores relate more to high-performing leaders (see Figure F.1). Once the research was completed, Future Management Systems mapped the WPI traits to Kirtman's Seven Competencies (see Figure F.2)

F.1 WPI Traits—Optimal Scores for High-Performing Leaders

60 and Above	50 and Above	40-60	50 and Below
• Achievement Orientation • Flexibility and Adaptability • Initiative • Independence • Innovation • Leadership Orientation • Persistence • Social Orientation	• Stress Tolerance • Self-Control	• Analytical Thinking	• Concern for Others • Cooperation • Rule Following • Dependability • Attention to Detail

Source: Kirtman (2014)

F.2 Mapping Kirtman's Seven Competencies to the WPI

WPI Traits	Kirtman's Seven Competencies
1. Persistence, Independence, Flexibility and Adaptability, Rule Following, Innovation, Attention to Detail, Initiative	1. Challenges the status quo
2. Stress Tolerance, Dependability, Concern for Others, Initiative, Leadership Orientation	2. Builds trust through clear communications and expectations
3. Achievement Orientation, Initiative, Leadership Orientation	3. Creates a commonly owned plan for success
4. Stress Tolerance, Self-Control, Concern for Others, Cooperation, Initiative, Achievement Orientation, Analytical Thinking, Innovation, Flexibility and Adaptability	4. Focuses on team over self
5. Achievement Orientation, Persistence, Initiative, Leadership Orientation, Cooperation, Dependability	5. Has a high sense of urgency for change and sustainable results in improving achievement
6. Cooperation, Social Orientation, Concern for Others, Stress Tolerance, Initiative, Leadership Orientation	6. Commits to improvement for self
7. Social Orientation, Achievement Orientation, Leadership Orientation, Initiative, Concern for Others	7. Builds external networks and partnerships

Figure F.3 displays WPI scores from our database of more than 9,000 educational leaders. The database includes principals, administrators, superintendents, and teacher leaders. The WPI self-assessment reflects behaviors, not skills or ability. It is only behavior at work, not personally at home. (The responses to the questions in the WPI vary based on a person's role and experience in education.) As you can see, no group except superintendents hit the 60 and above mark in achievement orientation. This means that educational leaders in general are more task than results oriented. Educators' behavior is mostly trying to get tasks completed that are sent to them from leaders above in the hierarchy.

F.3 Educator's Self-Assessed WPI Scores (2016-2021)

WPI Area	Administration	Teachers	Superintendents
Achievement Orientation (60+)	37	34	81
Persistence (60+)	51	39	64
Initiative (60+)	34	22	80
Leadership Orientation (60+)	39	27	88
Social Orientation (60+)	41	41	58
Cooperation (50-)	52	53	42
Concern for Others (50-)	59	71	36
Self-Control (50+)	42	42	43
Stress Tolerance (50+)	33	16	58
Flexibility and Adaptability (60+)	51	24	83
Dependability (50-)	29	39	39
Attention to Detail (50-)	25	34	19
Rule Following (50-)	23	23	13
Innovation (60+)	62	54	86
Analytical Thinking (40-60)	57	36	77
Independence (60+)	58	41	88

Figure F.3 shows the median scores of more than 2,800 people in education (collected between 2016 and 2021). We have broken down the scores based on the role of the respondent.

REFERENCES

Barnum, M. (2023, March). *Teacher turnover hits new highs across the U.S.* Chalkbeat. https://www.chalkbeat.org/2023/3/6/23624340/teacher-turnover-leaving-the-profession-quitting-higher-rate/

Billing, F., & De Smet, A. (2023, May 22). *What is talent management?* McKinsey & Company. https://www.mckinsey.com/featured-insights/mckinsey-explainers/what-is-talent-management

Bruno, R. (2018, June 20). When did the U.S. stop seeing teachers as professionals? *Harvard Business Review.* https://hbr.org/2018/06/when-did-the-u-s-stop-seeing-teachers-as-professionals

Bryant, J. (2023, March 2). *K-12 teachers are quitting. What would make them stay?* McKinsey & Company. https://www.mckinsey.com/industries/education/our-insights/k-12-teachers-are-quitting-what-would-make-them-stay

Cappelli, P., & Tavis, A. (2016, October). The performance management revolution. *Harvard Business Review.* https://hbr.org/2016/10/the-performance-management-revolution

CAST. (2018). *Universal design for learning guidelines version 2.2.* http://udlguidelines.cast.org

DeWitt, P. (2021, May 16). Stress, anxiety, initiative fatigue . . . oh my! Perhaps it's time to "de-implement"? *Education Week.* https://www.edweek.org/leadership/opinionstress-anxiety-initiative-fatigueoh-my-perhaps-its-time-to-de-implement/2021/05

DeWitt, P. (2022a) *De-Implementation: Creating the space to focus on what works.* Corwin.

DeWitt, P. (2022b, November 21). Stop wasting your time on school improvement plans that don't work. Try this instead. *Education Week.* https://www.edweek.org/leadership/opinion-stop-wasting-your-time-on-school-improvement-plans-that-dont-work-try-this-instead/2022/11

Ferlazzo, L. (2022, October 10). 8 ways COVID has changed some teachers forever. *Education Week.* https://www.edweek.org/teaching-learning/opinion-8-ways-covid-has-changed-some-teachers-forever/2022/10

Fullan, M. (2023, January 9). Why we can't escape the status quo in education. *Education Week.* https://www.edweek.org/leadership/opinion-why-we-cant-escape-the-status-quo-in-education/2023/01

Fullan, M., & Kirtman, L. (2019). *Coherent school leadership: Forging clarity from complexity.* ASCD.

Fullan, M., & Quinn, J. (2015). *Coherence: The right drivers in action for schools, districts, and systems.* Corwin.

Gill, J. (2021, February 19). *Yes, principals are that important.* Wallace Foundation. https://wallacefoundation.org/resource/articles/yes-principals-are-important

Glazer, R. (2018, August 8). It's time to ditch performance improvement plans. Here's why. *Forbes.* https://www.forbes.com/sites/robertglazer/2018/08/02/its-time-to-ditch-performance-improvement-plans-heres-why/

Kirtman, L. (2014). *Leadership and Teams: The missing piece of the educational reform puzzle.* Pearson Publishing.

Kirtman, L., & Fullan, M. (2016). *Leadership: Key competencies for whole system change.* Solution Tree.

Kurz, A., Reddy, L. A., Kettler, R. J., Glover, T. A., Velasquez, M. K., & Kirtman, L. (2020). Workstyle attributes and their relations to instructional coaching behaviours. *Professional Development in Education, 48*(4), 611–623. https://doi.org/10.1080/19415257.2020.1712450

Lencioni, P. (2005). *Overcoming the five dysfunctions of a team: A field guide.* Jossey-Bass.

Li, X., Bergin, C., & Olsen, A. A. (2022). Positive teacher-student relationships may lead to better teaching. *Learning and Instruction, 80*(6045), 101581. https://www.doi.org/10.1016/j.learninstruc.2022.101581

Martin, R. (2007, June 1). How successful leaders think. *Harvard Business Review.* https://hbr.org/2007/06/how-successful-leaders-think

Martin, R. (2022, March–April). The real secret to retaining talent. *Harvard Business Review.* https://hbr.org/2022/03/the-real-secret-to-retaining-talent

Mortensen, M., & Edmondson, A. (2023) Rethink your employee value proposition. *Harvard Business Review.* https://hbr.org/2023/01/rethink-your-employee-value-proposition

National Center for Education Statistics. (2023a). *Characteristics of public school teachers. Condition of education.* U.S. Department of Education, Institute of Education Sciences. https://nces.ed.gov/programs/coe/indicator/clr

National Center for Education Statistics. (2023b). *Public school expenditures. Condition of Education.* U.S. Department of Education, Institute of Education Sciences. https://nces.ed.gov/programs/coe/indicator/cmb

National Equity Project. (n.d.). *Educational equity definition.* Retrieved April 1, 2024, from nationalequityproject.org

Noguera, P., & Noguera, J. (2023, September 1). Creating clarity on equity in schools. ASCD https://ascd.org/el/articles/creating-clarity-on-equity-in-schools

Norris, K., & Wiley, K. (2023) It will take more than $60K salaries to solve the teacher shortage. *Education Week.* https://www.edweek.org/leadership/opinion-it-will-take-more-than-60k-salaries-to-solve-the-teacher-shortage/2023/03

Peetz, C. (2023, August 23). More superintendents are quitting as the school year begins. *Education Week.* https://www.edweek.org/leadership/more-superintendents-are-quitting-as-school-year-begins/2023/08

Schwartz, S. (2022, July 20). What is LETRS? Why one training is dominating "science of reading" efforts. *Education Week.* https://www.edweek.org/teaching-learning/letrs-program-teacher-training

Smith, S. (2018). *Ending the average in education: A study on the importance of student individuality.* Indigo Education Company. https://indigoeducationcompany.com/wp-content/uploads/2020/12/EndAvgPaper.pdf

Stearns, R. (2024). *2024 policy white paper: A student-centered approach to education.* Scaling Student Success.

Urdan, T., & Schoenfelder, E. (2006). Classroom effects on student motivation: Goal structures, social relationships, and competence beliefs. *Journal of School Psychology, 44*(5), 331–349. https://doi.org/10.1016/j.jsp.2006.04.003

Walker, T. (2022, February 12). Survey: Alarming number of educators may soon leave the profession. *NEA Today.* https://www.nea.org/nea-today/all-news-articles/survey-alarming-number-educators-may-soon-leave-profession

Walker, T. (2023, January 19). The truth about SEL? It works. *NEA Today.* https://www

.nea.org/nea-today/all-news-articles/truth-about-sel-it-works

Will, M. (2021, November 29). Efforts to toughen teacher evaluations show no positive impact on students. *Education Week*. https://www.edweek.org/teaching-learning/efforts-to-toughen-teacher-evaluations-show-no-positive-impact-on-students/2021/11

Wolf, M. (2021, June 14). *Lift up teachers and treat them as professionals*. EdNC. https://www.ednc.org/perspective-lift-up-teachers-and-treat-them-as-professionals/

INDEX